Our Partners

Centre for Youth and Social Development
E-1 Institutional Area, Gangadhar Meher Marg,
Bhubaneswar, 751013 (Orissa)
Email: cysdbbsr@sancharnet.in
cysdbbsr@vsnl.net

All India Disaster Mitigation Institute
411, Sakar Five,
Near Nataraj Cinema, Ashram Road,
Ahmedabad - 380009 (Gujarat)
E-mail : dmi@icenet.co.in

Center for World Solidarity
12-13-438, Street No.1, Tarnaka,
Secunderabad - 500 017 (Andhra Pradesh)
E-mail: info@cwsy.org

Research Coordinator : Dr. G. Palanithurai

Research Team : Dr. G. Uma, Research officer
Dr. R.P. Natarajamurthy, Research Assistant
Ms. Sivagama Sundari, Research Assistant
Ms. Elizabeth Mathew, Research Assistant
Mr. P. Gabendran, Computing and Documentation Assistant

About the Research Coordinator

Prof. Ganapathi Palanithurai, Coordinator in Rajiv Gandhi Chair, Gandhigram Rural Institute, presently heads the Department of Political Science and Development Administration, Gandhigram Rural University, Tamil Nadu. He is also Associated with Centre Planning Commission, State Planning Commission of Tamil Nadu, Population Foundation of India, the Ford Foundation, UNICEF, Rajiv Gandhi Foundation, CAPART, Ministry of Rural Development and DANIDA (Danish-Indo Development Agency) in specific areas of activities in connection with empowerment of people.

Prof. Palanithurai has to his credit fifty-two books and ninty-five articles on three major areas, namely, legislative behaviour, ethnicity and Panchayati Raj system. He was recipient of Fellowship from Sastri Indo-Canadian Institute, New Delhi and World Academy of Art and Science, USA. He is the Chairman of the Tamil Nadu Council for Sustainable Livelihoods. He was a visiting Fellow in the MiGill University, Canada in 1989. He is a member of the expert committee constituted by the Government of Tamil Nadu to monitor the training programme for local body leaders. He is a member of High Level Committee headed by the Minister of Panchayati Raj, Government of Tamil Nadu for further devolution of powers.

Panchayats in Disaster Preparedness and Management

Gujarat, Orissa, Andhra Pradesh and Tamil Nadu

[With Successful Case Studies]

G. Palanithurai

Supported by

Action Aid India International

CONCEPT PUBLISHING COMPANY, NEW DELHI-110059

Cataloging in Publication Data—DK
Courtesy: D.K. Agencies (P) Ltd. <docinfo@dkagencies.com>

Palanithurai, G. (Ganapathy), 1953-
Panchayats in disaster preparedness and management : Gujarat, Orissa, Andhra Pradesh and Tamil Nadu : with successful case studies / G. Palanithurai.
p. cm.
Includes bibliographical references (p.).
Includes index.
ISBN 13: 9788180694790
ISBN 10: 8180694798

1. Natural disasters—India. 2. Emergency management—India—Societies, etc. 3. Disaster relief—India. 4. Disaster victims—Rehabilitation—India. 5. Panchayat—India. I. Title.

DDC 363.347 095 4 22

This publication is the outcome of the Project Report on the "Role of Panchayats in Disaster Preparedness and Management in four states in India—Gujarat, Orissa, Andhra Pradesh and Tamil Nadu" supported by Action Aid India International, Chennai.

ISBN-13: 978-81-8069-479-0
ISBN-10: 81-8069-479-8

First Published 2009

Published and Printed by
Ashok Kumar Mittal
Concept Publishing Company
A/15-16, Commercial Block, Mohan Garden
New Delhi-110059 (INDIA)

Phone : 25351460, 25351794
Fax : 091-11-25357103
Email : publishing@conceptpub.com

Acknowledgements

It is our role to look at issues from the perspective of the poor, marginalized, women and dalits more preciously and specifically in all circumstances how they are perceived, placed, helped and facilitated to lead a decent human life with human dignity in all unequal society, socially and economically. Disasters whether it is natural or manmade will affect the poor in a large measure and it is painful for them to regain their old position in the process of relief, rehabilitation and reconstruction as they have been made mere dole receivers and they have no say in any decision making. Organizations, institutions involved in all those activities have incorporated a clause in their document that stakeholders' participation is a must in the process of all activities. But on the ground it is absolutely negated. In this context, a study was designed to investigate the role of Panchayats in disaster preparedness and disaster management with the support of Action Aid India. To complete any study many individuals and organizations' collaboration is an imperative. Hence, we have three partners, namely, Centre for Youth and Social Development (CYSD), Bhubaneshwar, Orissa, All India Disaster Mitigation Institute (AIDMI), Ahmedabad, Gujarat, Centre for World Solidarity (CWS), Secundrabad, Andhra Pradesh, and they have helped us to undertake intensive field-work and interaction with different stakeholders from the field to policy makers. In all the states, they have extended assistance in immeasurable terms and for which I registered my gratitude to them. Further, the stake-holders, Panchayat leaders, representatives of NGOs, funding agencies, government officials were frank, open and objective in responding to our requests and queries. They need special mention here as they shared their valuable time with us. Hence, I record my thanks to them. Thirdly, the research team worked in this project involved and immersed in this project with a sense of dedication and commitment which brought tons of evidences and data. They worked untiringly till the completion of the project. We can write series of articles with the collected data for this work. Against this I express my indebtedness to them. Fourthly, the participants of the workshop from the four States have contributed immensely in the validation workshop. I place on record, my thanks to them. Fifthly, my staff in the department and in other projects have cooperated to complete the task and for which I express my deep sense of gratitude. Finally, I register my thanks to Action Aid India for supporting this study.

Gandhigram

G. Palanithurai

Executive Summary

It is a mantra that "stakeholders participation", "peoples participation", "participatory democracy", "participatory development" being used in a society which is known for its structural divisions based on caste and class and in which patriarchy has strongly embedded in the society. While analysing these principles from conceptualization to operationalization one would find the severity of resistance at different levels considering the nature of the institutions and organizations. It is nothing but mere empowering people and building the capacity of the people. When we refer people it refers to the marginalized, women, deprived, adivasis and dalits. The self-respect and self-dignity are the most essential requirements for the poor to retain their status in the society. No doubt, it is a process of struggle and initiatives have to be from the above starting from the Constitution and from below starting from the community. In India, the Constitution has granted power to the people through the 73rd Amendment to establish a participatory, inclusive and a gender sensitive governance, development and administration at the grassroots. In many of the places communities reject the concessions extended by the constitution because of the structural barriers created by the caste and patriarchal system in India. Against this background, the study was undertaken to investigate as to what extent the Panchayats are involved in disaster preparedness and management in four states—Gujarat, Orissa, Andhra Pradesh and Tamil Nadu in India. We were clear right from the beginning that our research is not going to be a mere theoretical analysis. With this view, a number of case studies were conducted. Our primary focus has been in the manner in which constitutional Panchayat synergises with traditional Panchayat and community in disaster management, the way in which constitutional panchayat managed disaster. When we say that there are findings, the question arises where do we want to go?, if it is related to polity, then two clear-cut options are there. The first option is about sensitizing policy makers, while the second is about the extent to which the Panchayats have the power and capability to tackle the problems at the local level. In course of our research, we have attempted to analyse the perspectives of the organizations, institutions, government on relief and rehabilitation and the involvement of the stakeholders in relief, rehabilitation and reconstruction activities. It is proved beyond doubt that the states are in union in operationalising the new framework of involving people and communities through Panchayats not only in development activities but also in disaster mitigation. Though it is emphasized much, there is no systematic effort to involve and empower the people as the main stakeholders. Our system at the top and the middle always believe that technology and resources from the West alone will work for the development. People, that too, the poor are seen and perceived as beneficiaries, dole receivers and petitioners. They are involved nominally. It is the mindset that tells everyone that people never be useful and have no capacity to manage themselves. Hence, whether it is development or disaster, it is always the work of the bureaucracies and policy makers.

Content

List of Tables

List of Boxes

List of Abbreviations and Acronyms

AIDMI	-	All India Disaster Management Institute
ANMs	-	Auxiliary Nurse Midwives
APL	-	Above Poverty Line
BDO	-	Block Development Officer
BPL	-	Below Poverty Line
CASA	-	Church's Auxiliary for Social Action
CBOs	-	Community Based Organizations
CCP	-	Community Contingency Plan
CIDA	-	Canadian International Development Agency
CLAP	-	Committee for Legal Aid to the Poor
CPDP	-	Centre for People's Action for Disaster Preparedness
CREED	-	Center for Rural Education and Economic Development
CRS	-	Catholic Relief Service
CYSD	-	Centre for Youth and Social Development
DC	-	Disciple Centre
DDO	-	District Development Officer
DMT	-	Disaster Management Teams
DOART	-	Deportation Assessment and Reporting Technology
DWCRA	-	Development of Women and Children in Rural Areas
EWRs	-	Elected Women Representatives
EWS	-	Early Warning Systems
GCERT	-	Gujarat Centre for Educational Research and Training
GIDM	-	Gujarat Institute of Disaster Management

GoG	-	Government of Gujarat
GOs	-	Government Orders
GP	-	Gram Panchayat
GPRS	-	General Pocket Radio Service
GSDMA	-	Gujarat State Disaster Management Authority
HAM	-	Amateur Radio (Wireless Interference)
HUDCO	-	Housing and Urban Development Corporation
ICT	-	Information Communication Technology
IDNDR	-	International Decade for Natural Disaster Reduction
INGOs	-	International Non Governmental Organizations
KMVS	-	Kutch Mahila Vikas Sangathan
KSSS	-	Kotar Social Service Society
MLA	-	Member of Legislative Assembly
MPDOs	-	Mandal Panchayats Development Officers
MRO	-	Mandal Revenue Officer
NCC	-	National Cadet Corps
NCRC	-	NGOs Coordination Resource Center
NGOs	-	Non-Governmental Organizations
ODMM	-	Organizations of Disaster Management and Mitigation
OHT	-	Over Head Tank
OSDMA	-	Orissa State Disaster Mitigation Authority
PESA	-	Panchayat Extension Service Act
PHC	-	Primary Health Centre
PMSSS	-	Pondicherry Multipurpose Social Service Society
PRA	-	Participatory Rural Appraisal
PREPARE	-	Indian Rural Reconstruction and Disaster Response Service
PRI	-	Panchayati Raj Institutions
PRO	-	Public Relation Officer
PWD	-	Public Works Department
RD	-	Rural Development
RDO	-	Revenue Divisional Officer
RMP	-	Registered Medical Practitioner
SC	-	Scheduled Castes
SCARF	-	Schizophrenia Research Foundation (India)
SDC	-	Swizz Development Corporation
SDRN	-	State Disaster Management Network

SECURE	-	Socio-Economic Cultural Enlistment in Rural Environment
SEWA	-	Self Employed Women Association
SHGs	-	Self Help Groups
SIRD	-	State Institute of Rural Development
SRC	-	State Resource Centre
ST	-	Scheduled Tribes
SVAS	-	An NGO
TNTRC	-	Tamil Nadu Tsunami Resource Centre
TRRC	-	Tsunami Relief and Rehabilitation Coordination
TT	-	Tetanus Toxide
TV	-	Television
UN	-	United Nations
UNDP	-	United Nations Development Programme
UNICEF	-	United Nations International Children's Emergency Fund
UNNATI	-	An Organization for Development Education
VAO	-	Village Administrative Officer
VDO	-	Village Development Officer
VHAK	-	Voluntary Health Association of Kanyakumari
VKC	-	Village Knowledge Centre
VRO	-	Village Revenue Officer

About the book

This book examines the role of Panchayats in disaster management in India. Based on an action research carried out in four states—Gujarat, Orissa, Andhra Pradesh and Tamil Nadu, it analyses the response of the communities and Panchayats towards tsunami and other natual disasters, with specific reference to the issues of gender and exclusion in relief as well as rehabilitation work.

Also, it deals with the communication system in the entire coastal area for early warning messages to the communities, the interface between traditional and constitutional Panchayats, the disaster management policy, and relief codes from the perspective of local grassroots governance. The relief, rehabilitation and reconstruction activities undertaken by government institutions and NGOs have been evaluated as well. The book is useful for researchers, policy makers and development workers.

1

Introduction

India, in the post-Independence era, witnessed for the first time in 2004, the most devastating spectacle of the Tsunami which caused a great damage to the lives and properties of the people in the coastal areas. The Andaman and Nicobar islands, the costal districts of Andhra Pradesh, Tamil Nadu, Pondicherry and Kerala were the affected regions. As per the report of the Government of India, 10,881 people lost their lives, 57,924 persons were reported missing and 6,913 were injured. In Tamil Nadu, over 8,010 deaths were reported. Of the thirteen coastal districts affected, Nagapattinam, where 6,065 people died, was the worst affected. Over 828 died in Kanyakumari District and 617 were reported dead in Cuddalore District.

No doubt damage was enormous in Tamil Nadu and donor responses were equally impressive in terms of commitment to reconstruct the Tsunami affected areas by their funding. Activities were initiated for relief by the NGOs, INGOs and government departments and they were well coordinated through the District Administration. Subsequently, rehabilitation activities were designed through a framework evolved by the Government of Tamil Nadu. Activities were in full swing. Still, after one year of relief and rehabilitation activities by the institutions, organizations and government departments in spending huge money, lives of the people in the coastal districts were miserable, vulnerable and inhuman. People have been made voiceless, and treated like mere petitioners and beneficiaries, orphans and dole receivers. People have not been allowed to claim their dignity, self-esteem and self-respect. It was obvious that the people have lost confidence and they had been oriented to look for assistance from the external agencies even for a small disaster. That was the way in which people have been oriented by all the agencies by their good actions. This was witnessed in the field where reconstruction activities were on.

The perspectives and frameworks of donors, their affiliates, their network partners, and local organizations have changed the social dynamics and dismantled the structures created by the communities by the activities carried out by the organizations with their own perspectives. The government, for its own share, developed a framework to keep its control over both the community and the agencies which have come to work for relief and rehabilitation. The government of Tamil Nadu issued a variety of orders on all aspects of relief and rehabilitation by which it declared itself the major player and the responsible player in relief and rehabilitation and allowed the NGOs to carry out activities and help the government within the framework created by the government. The relationship between the government and the NGOs gave the impression that the government was the master and the NGOs were the contractors to carry out the activities. Knowing fully well the limitations of the panchayats created through provisions of the Constitution, many of the donor agencies have made good use of the powers of traditional panchayats as they are vibrant in their relationship with the community. As a result, the constitutional Panchayats were not actively and legitimately involved in relief, rehabilitation and reconstruction activities. The Panchayat Presidents expressed their displeasure over the neglect of the constitutional Panchayats in disaster relief and management activities.

There was no woman in the traditional panchayats and yet these panchayats were promoted as agents of relief and rehabilitation activities by NGOs, INGOs and the Government. It was democratic, in a limited sense and it exhibited its vibrancy in controlling and managing the community through the social laws evolved over a period of time. But where were the women in the Traditional Panchayats! Due to heavy flow of funds and doles, even the traditional Panchayat leaders were frequently changed because of the pressure of the community. In many places, the traditional panchayats behaved like a ruler and they controlled the communities and the communities had no voice at all. What we saw as the inequity issue in other communities could be seen among the fisher folk also. The rich-poor divide was also visible. The poor had no voice. They sought the help of others to get their grievances redressed. In certain areas the church played a predominant role in deciding matters by pushing both traditional Panchayat and constitutional Panchayat leaders out. Sometimes, even the government officials had to accept the role of the church to carry out their activities. That was the kind of predominant role the church had assumed. Even though the fisherfolk live in a Panchayat area, it was never connected with the other communities and the constitutionally created Panchayats. The relief and rehabilitation activities brought about some changes in the lives of the fisher communities, but all of them were not positive. NGOs were constructing houses but not creating habitat. Community consultation, Panchayat involvement in the process of relief and reconstruction were abysmal. The equity issue was a major problem which had been created due to uneven allocations of resources by the agencies for relief and rehabilitation activities. The poor found that their livelihood itself had been affected as they were dependent on fishing. But they were not considered for relief and rehabilitation. In many places relief activities were donor-driven and supply-driven not demand-driven.

Conflicts within community, conflicts between communities were intense. The conflicts arose out of the distribution of relief and rehabilitation packages. Organizations showed their special characteristics and, as a result, the organic link of the issue affecting the community had not been effectively addressed. Issues had to be seen from the perspective of the sector and area integrally and not in isolation. It was unfortunate that they were seen in isolation. Women were made to be visible in the process of relief and rehabilitation activities as tokens and not in real terms. Dalits and farmers were neglected in the relief phase. After a prolonged fight, they were included. The fragile bargaining strength of the NGOs made them succumb to the pressure of the government. The NGOs were seen as contractors as they were treated by the government as institutions and organizations to carry out activities within the framework laid down by the government. The NCRC, which had been created with lofty ideals, was made a mouthpiece of the government departments rather than acting as the coordinating agency to consolidate the activities of the NGOs. Transparency and accountability, which are being talked about, became casualty. Absolutely there was no downward accountability on the part of the government, NGOs, INGOs and others. Realistically speaking, the community had got the energy and it proved it in the first two days after the Tsunami by removing the dead bodies and clearing the villages without expecting anybody's help. After the fourth day the entire relief and rehabilitation activities were taken away from the community. A system had to be placed on the ground to meet any eventuality, but it was not happening. A lot of innovative activities were carried out by small organizations with the involvement of the communities. But they were not taken into account and properly documented.

Ultimately, the people were treated as beneficiaries and as a result, if there were any disaster in future (it should not happen) people would look for help from external agencies and the government. To sum up, as a result of all the relief and rehabilitation activities, communities had been made to lose their self-dignity, self-esteem and self-confidence. Against this background this research study was designed to investigate as to what extent the constitutional Panchayats could be involved in relief, rehabilitation and reconstruction activities.

New Panchayati Raj System

Panchayati Raj Institutions in India have emerged as governance institutions at grassroots to achieve economic development and social justice after the enactment of the 73rd Amendment to the Constitution of India. It is the third tier of governance created at the district level, block level and village level with a view to make local administration responsive, responsible and representative. These new Panchayati Raj Institutions have to function as little republics not as little kingdoms as the character of our society is feudal, hierarchical and patriarchal. It has got the potential to transform the representative democracy to participatory democracy through the vibrant functioning of Gram Sabha. It has to function under the collective leadership rather than individual leader and for which statutory functional committees are created. To address the question of exclusion, provisions have been given to reserve seats not less than one-third to women and proportionate to the population to SC and ST at all levels of governance in Panchayats. To work on the demand and vision of the people, planning at micro level is ensured through the District Planning Committee. To ensure regular flow of funds State Finance Commissions make periodical recommendations. Thus the new Panchayats have the potential to provide opportunity to the communities to lead a decent and dignified human life by protecting their self-dignity. It also enables the hitherto excluded to be included in governance. By stepping into Panchayati Raj Institutions, communities can work for livelihood security, economic development and social justice.

Role of Panchayats

The Panchayati Raj Institutions have a significant place in the process of disaster preparedness and management. The functionaries of the Panchayat Raj Institution involved in disaster management can train the people to face disasters through the community initiatives; keep people in safer places and maintain proper administration of relief in emergencies; mobilize the people and sensitize them to have enough courage and preparedness to face the situation; reduce the extent of loss and damage due to the disaster; assess the damages caused by the disaster; take initiative to develop micro plan for reconstruction; initiate long-term measures to prevent or minimize the intensity of disasters.

Every Gram Panchayat will have a committee exclusively for disaster management. They have to be fully trained and they have to be involved in all disaster management activities. Whether the committee has been constituted in every Gram Panchayat and trained is a question. In certain select gram panchayats in Tamil Nadu training was given even before the tsunami struck the coastal areas and those panchayats had their own advantages of the training in preparedness and saved the lives of many and reduced the material loss also.

Synergy between the Constitutional Panchayats and Community Panchayats

India has a rich tradition of village self-governance evolved through social laws. Social laws are more powerful than the Constitutional laws. In rural areas different forms of community Panchayats were functioning in different parts of India. Community Panchayats fulfil many of the needs of the local community. Most of the common properties of the villages were still controlled by the community. Particularly during disasters these Panchayats were able to generate collective action to save people. Hence, community norms, procedures and practices got primacy at the grassroots level and the constitutional authorities were not able to bring a radical transformation at the community level. As a result these community Panchayats still hold considerable control over communities. Wherever the leadership at the Panchayat level both in Constitutional Panchayats and Community Panchayats has got commitment, understanding, maturity and vision, one will find synergy between the two and they work for the betterment of the communities by using all the opportunities that are coming from the Central and State governments through the development schemes and programmes. In the absence of the above, in many panchayats, conflict and tension prevail in the community due to conflict between the Constitutional Panchayats and Community Panchayats. Constitutional Panchayats were not drawn from heaven. They were also functioning in the communities and hence they have the characteristics of the Community Panchayats even though the structures were created to fulfil the mandate of the constitutional provision. Community Panchayats were also transforming themselves to be democratic because of the influence of the external agencies. Both could play a complementary role in delivering services to the people. In responding to tsunami, Community Panchayats had a greater role than the Constitutional Panchayats. Constitutional Panchayats took active role wherever they were headed by committed leaders. In the process of relief and rehabilitation activities, Community Panchayats have transformed their characters by including women into their governance units. In the same way Constitutional Panchayats have learnt how to work with multiple organizations in a crisis situation.

Government and Civil Society Organizations

In the absence of relief code and disaster management policy, the state government had created a framework for relief and rehabilitation under which the state took its dominant, regulatory, supervisory role and civil society organizations undertook the activities as implementing agencies. Moreover, the lessons learnt in the past have not been used. India also has got rich experience in disaster mitigation but they are not being properly used. Mahatma Gandhi himself had undertaken relief and rehabilitation works which is known as "the Gandhian Perspective of Disaster Management". In Tamil Nadu after tsunami, District Administration was fully empowered to take decision and hence the confusions seen in Gujarat, Orissa and Maharashtra were avoided. The whole relief activities were managed in a decentralized way under the leadership of many ministers and rural development officials. The approach was totally decentralized but not integrated with local bodies.

Panchayats' Role in Addressing Equity Issues

Panchayats as institutions of governance have the potential to allow the stakeholders to claim their dues and entitlements as rights. They provided opportunity to women, Dalit and other segments of the rural society in Panchayat governance. The representatives can play a meaningful role in the whole process of decision making and allocation of resources. It requires training and proper capacity building for the Panchayat leaders. In Gram Sabha all transactions of Panchayats have to be placed for public perusal and approval. If the members of Gram Sabha were vigilant, informed and empowered, they will stake their rightful claims. Panchayats have to address the issues of exclusion. Necessarily panchayat leaders should be sensitive on the issues of gender and exclusion. Panchayats have got the power to prepare a contingent plan for disaster mitigation and reconstruction in which the special component for Dalit and women could be incorporated and implemented.

Experience from Disaster for Panchayat's Role

We had earthquake, super cyclone, tsunami, floods, drought and fire in different states in different magnitude and for which Centre and State governments responded through their resource allocation for relief and rehabilitation activities. At micro level, a large number of institutions and organizations were involved in activities with the support of government, NGOs and INGOs. After the enactment of the 73rd Amendment, Constitutional Panchayats were in position. From the experience of the states in responding to the natural disaster, a perspective could be developed for future action. It will strengthen the local organizations, communities and institutions and reduce the risks through their preparedness.

Why This Study?

Of course, India has an act, institutions, organizations at the Centre for disaster management. At the state level barring a few states, many did not have a perspective policy and relief code. Till date Tamil Nadu has not evolved relief code and disaster management policy and act. At the ground very little has been done in terms of strengthening the institutions for delivery of services and empowering the people. In every occurrence of disaster, all outside agencies including government reached the community only after a minimum of two days. It was only the Village Panchayat and communities manage themselves till the arrival of external agencies for disaster management. It is necessary to strengthen the local communities through the Panchayats to face any disaster by proper capacity building for disaster preparedness and assigning due and legitimate role to prevent large scale damages to human lives and materials. Against this background a study was designed to investigate as to what extent panchayats performed the role in disaster preparedness and management in a few states, namely Gujarat, Orissa, Andhra Pradesh and Tamil Nadu. Tsunami is the context, but the study goes beyond in other states as *ex post facto* research to bring to light what has to be done for mutual learning based on the experiences of the other states and to strengthen the local institutions for effective disaster preparedness and risk reduction.

The following are the objectives of the study:

(a) To study the response of the communities and the Panchayats towards Tsunami and other natural disasters in the first few days till the strong entry of NGOs and Government Departments;
(b) To study the issues of gender and exclusion in relief and rehabilitation activities and to evolve a strategy to deal with them;
(c) To evolve a communication system in the entire coastal area for communicating early warning system;
(d) To study the linkage between traditional panchayats and constitutional Panchayats in relief and rehabilitation activities;
(e) To evolve strategy to strengthen the constitutional Panchayats from the perspectives of preparedness;
(f) To study the role of Disaster Management Committee at the Gram Panchayat level and its linkages with Block Disaster Management Committee and District Disaster Management Committee;
(g) To evolve strategies to create preparedness among the community and Panchayats in the entire coastal area;
(i) To assess the efforts of the institutions in building up disaster preparedness among the local institutions;
(j) To study the process of interaction between the traditional Panchayats and the constitutional Panchayats;
(k) To study the role of Women and Dalits in relief and rehabilitation activities;
(l) To study the downward accountability in the entire relief and rehabilitation activities;

(m) To study the relief code and disaster management policy from the perspective of grassroots institutions; and to assess to what extent the lessons learnt in the past in handling disaster have been used for rehabilitation work after the tsunami.

Methodology

This study was based on intensive fieldwork carried out in four states, namely Orissa, Andhra Pradesh, Gujarat and Tamil Nadu. The above said four states were affected by flood, cyclone, tsunami and earthquake. In case of Andhra Pradesh flood in Godavari was a regular phenomenon. In case of Orissa, flood, cyclone and drought have occurred continuously for the last ten years. In the case of Gujarat earthquake ravaged the state. Both primary and secondary data have been collected and used in this study. Primary data collected through direct interview with the Gram Panchayat Presidents, Gram Panchayat Members, Block Panchayat Chairman and Members, District Panchayat Chairman and Members, Self Help Group Members, representatives of Non-Governmental Organizations, INGOs, UNDP, Government Officials and Community leaders. Focus group discussions were held among traditional Panchayat leaders, self help group members, fisher folk, youth of fisher folk, dalits (both men and women separately) and farmers. Secondary data were collected through reviewing existing literature on disaster response activities. Training manuals, pamphlets, NGOs and INGOs activity reports, Government publications and NGOs, INGOs publications were used extensively. To document the best practices, intensive case studies were done in a few Panchayats in all the four states. Informal discussions were held among them and cases were well documented. Apart from Government Orders, Relief and Rehabilitation Code, Disaster Management Policy and Panchayat Act of four states have been reviewed.

Study Area

In select four states, namely Andhra Pradesh, Gujarat, Orissa and Tamil Nadu, highly disaster-prone districts, three in number were selected based on the intensity of the disaster. In the select three districts, blocks were chosen based on the intensively of the damage within the disaster affected district and, among the block, gram panchayats were chosen based on the following criteria: (a) Gram panchayats should be women headed;

(b) Gram panchayats should be Dalit headed; (c) Severity of the devastation; (d) Strong preference of traditional panchayats; (e) Following are the details of the field covered in this study:

Table 1.1: Details of States, Districts, Blocks, Gram Panchayats Selected for this Study

S. No.	*Name of the State*	*Name of the Districts*	*Name of the Blocks*	*Name of the Village Panchayat*
1.	Tamil Nadu	1. Kanyakumari	Killiur	Midalam
			Agastheeswaram	1. Kovalam 2. Leepuram
			Rajakkamangalam	1. Manakudi 2. Pallam
			Kurundankode	1. Colachel 2. Simon Colony
		2. Nagapattinam	Sirkali	1. Vanagiri 2. Manikka Pangu 3. Kaveri Poompattinam
			Keelayur	1. P.R. Puram 2. Kameshwaram
			Cuddalore	1. Gunduuppalavadi 2. Pachankuppam 3. Cuddalore
			Parangipettai	1. Pudhu Kuppam 2. Samiyarpettai 3. Chinnor Pudhu Pettai
2.	Gujarat	1. Surendra Nagar	Vaduvam Block	1. Timba 2. Duduvada
		2. Patna	Rathanpur	1. Najupura
			Santhalpur	1. Fangli 2. Khavada
		3. Buji	Buji	1. Kaladi 2. Dador 3. Thaladi
3	Andhra Pradesh	1. Nellore	Kota Vaakadu	Kotha Pattinam Pudirayatheru
		2. Khammam	Burugambadu Kukkanoor	1. Petharaikudam Chiravali
		3. East Godavari	Mamidakuduru Kapeleswaram	Karavaku Addanki Vari lanka
4.	Orissa	1. Jagatsinghpur	1. Ragunathpur 2. Balikuda	 Olabole
		2. Cuttack 3. Puri	Niyali Nimapura	Ranikola

Details of Interaction with NGOs, INGOs and the Government Officials in Each State

Tamil Nadu

INGOs

The research team had in-depth discussion with the representatives of United Nations Development Programme (UNDP), World Vision, SCARF—India, Concern World Wide, German Agro Action, CARE India, Catholic Relief Services, CARITAS India, CASA, NCRC, Covenant Centre for Development, and The Hunger Project.

Non-Governmental Organizations

The research team interacted with the representatives of the Trust for Village Self Governance, Voluntary Health Association of Kanyakumari (VHAK), Disciple Centre (DC), Karunalaya, PREPARE, SEVALAYA, SCORD, BLESS, ASSEFFA, WORLD, CREED, NANGAL, and Kottar Social Service Society (KSSS).

Governmental Officials

Following officials were contacted and interacted, Officials involved in relief and rehabilitation, Project officers of DRDA—Cuddalore and Nagapattinam, Tamil Nadu Tsunami Resource Centre (TNTRC), Block Development Officials, Revenue Development Officials.

Elected Representatives

Following elected representatives of the people were involved in the discussion to get to know the details of activities: District Panchayat Chairman, Gram Panchayat Leaders, Block Panchayat Chairman.

Orissa

INGOs

The research team had discussion with the Representatives in inter Agency Group, Action Aid, UNDP, and Red Cross.

Non-Governmental Organizations

The research team held discussions with the CYSD, ODMM, Utkal Seva Samaj, CLAP, Navajothi, Rural Welfare Institute and Vikas.

Government Official

The following officials were contacted to get to know the details of disaster management: Officials from Orissa State Disaster Management Authority (OSDMA)—Mr. Gyana Dass, Officials from District Collectorate, and Block Development Officer.

Andhra Pradesh

INGOs

The research team held discussion with the representatives of Center for World Solidarity.

Non-Governmental Organizations

The research team held discussion with Speak India, SECURE, and SVAS (Samata).

Governmental Officials

The following government officials were contacted for discussion by the research team: Mandal Revenue Officer, Mandal Agriculture Officer,

Mandal Veterinary Officer, Mandal Engineer, and Mandal Development Official.

Gujarat

INGOs

The research team had discussion with the representatives of Oxfam, AIDMI, and Aga Khan Rural Support Programme.

Non-Governmental Organizations

Representatives of the civil society organization have been contacted for this study. Discussions were held with the representatives of the following organizations SEWA, Kutch Nav Nirman Abhiyan, SETU, and UNNATI.

Governmental Officials

Officials of the following organizations have been contacted and interacted with them: HUDCO, BHAD, DDO, Praful Harshe IAS, and the Medical Officer.

Chapterization of the Book

The book has seven chapters. The first chapter introduces the problem and spells out the methodological nuances adopted for collection of data and analysis. The second chapter deals with the perspectives of the organizations, institutions, government on relief and rehabilitation activities. The third chapter presents the details of relief, rehabilitation and reconstruction activities of the government, donor agencies. The fourth chapter brings to light the involvement of stakeholders in relief and rehabilitation activities. The fifth chapter discusses the role of panchayats in disaster management and interface between the traditional Panchayats and the constitutional Panchayats. The sixth chapter analyses ways and means to strengthen community and Panchayat preparedness to manage disaster mitigation. The seventh chapter contains the findings, conclusions and recommendations.

2

Perspectives of the Organizations, Institutions, Government on Relief and Rehabilitation

This chapter attempts to provide an overview of the perspectives of the organizations, institutions and the government on relief, rehabilitation and reconstruction activities. Such an overview is necessary to understand the issues involved in disasters with a view, to strengthen the delivery mechanism in relief, rehabilitation and reconstruction in future. Based on the above this chapter identifies the gaps and suggests ways and means to fill them up. The perspective will be on the following aspects:

(a) Disaster management ethics;
(b) Centre-State fund sharing;
(c) International funding for disaster response;
(d) Environmental preparedness and recovery (Institutional role);
(e) Disaster Development Link (Institutional enforcement agency);
(f) Informatics for disaster management;
(g) Use of fresh BPL list;
(h) Dead body identification and death certificates;
(i) Dissemination of information regarding warnings;
(j) Participation in the policy making;
(k) Gender dimension;
(l) Provision for animals; and
(m) Special provision for children.

The perspectives of the organizations, institutions, government on relief and rehabilitation were analyzed statewise and finally, conclusions have been drawn.

Orissa

Orissa Disaster History

Orissa is divided into 30 districts, 314 blocks, 5263 Gram Panchayats and 50,972 revenue villages. It has 155,707 sq. km of total area. 87 per cent of the people live in rural areas and mostly depend on agriculture for their livelihood. The total cultivable land is 65.59 lakh hectares and out of which only 24.69 per cent is irrigated and rest is rain-fed. The primary sector remains unproductive due to lack of irrigation, infrastructure and proneness to natural calamities. The major disasters faced by Orissa are floods, cyclone, drought, heat wave, fire and pollution. Over a period of a century Orissa has faced 90 years of major and minor disasters.

From 1843 to 1993, Orissa faced 50 major floods. Floods of high disaster occurred in 1896, 1920, 1926, 1934, 1940, 1955, 2001, 2003 (Mahanadi River System) and 1881, 1894, 1907, 1927, 1940 and 1943 in Bhahmani and Baitarani river systems. The maximum frequency of the occurrence of floods of all magnitude is experienced in two phases of the monsoon season from 21st July to 7th August and from 21st August to 7th December. After Hirakud Dam came in 1956, Mahanadi was in control for some years but the frequency of floods has increased significantly since 1965.

After flood, Orissa is frequented by Cyclone. Very severe cyclones affected Orissa Coast on 8th October 1948, 1971 and 1999. On all these occasions, the wind speed was more than 120 to 180 km/h. The speed depended on the length of wind's way, the depression or the distance covered over the sea before it reached the coast. In Orissa, the maximum number of cyclones occur during the south-west monsoon period, followed by the post-monsoon period of the north-east monsoon and the pre-monsoon period. The average lifespan of a cyclone is about six days from the time when it is formed until it dissipates. The super cyclones (1999) involved winds up to 300 km/h, tidal waves reaching 7-10 metres which came in 10-15 kms inland and incessant rain (447-995) for 48 hours.

The third most regular visitor to Orissa is drought. Orissa has seen a very severe famine in 1866 when 1.5 lakh people died of starvation. Orissa belongs to a tropical savannah type climate. The southwest monsoon remains active from 10th June in coastal plains and from 1st

July in the whole state. There is a falling trend in rainfall in Orissa since 1950. While all districts are suffering from deficient rain at least once in every three to four years, some districts are annually affected by drought. The annual rainfall in whole of Orissa in average is 1482.2 mm. with a plus or minus 19 per cent deviation, the situation can be managed. Between 1965 and 1987 Orissa has witnessed seven droughts, as there was 20.4 per cent to 35.86 per cent deviation. A study has revealed that due to deforestation rainfall has declined in the upper reaches of Mahanadi during 1946-1976. Deforestation of the hot wet tropical rain forests in Dandakaranya has most probably adversely affected rainfall in the Kalahandi Plateau further westwards.

Just like droughts the frequency of heat waves is also rising. The worst heat wave in recent history affected the state in 1988 when 2000 people perished in 16 districts of the state. Heat waves seem to have a direct connection with global warming, deforestation and vehicular emissions. Fire incidents are as devasting as heat wave in Orissa. A report in May 1990 said that property worth Rs. 50,000 was gutted everyday in an average of 10 accidents. Fire mishaps have been on the rise. In 1975, 1718 accidents were reported while it was 6712 in 1989.

Last but not the least earthquake has not yet shown its furry in the state. However, Bhubaneshwar, Puri and the critical Hirakud Dam fall within the moderate damage risk zone. The city of Ahmedabad is also located in the same zone which was badly affected by 2001 earthquake.

With respect to Government of Orissa, it did not have standardized systems and structures, delivery mechanisms during emergency before 1999 super cyclone. The Government of Orissa depended more on officers concerned at different levels and was less institutionalized. There was lack of clarity on the roles, responsibilities and accountability before 1999 Super Cyclone. Similarly, there was lack of people's participation and they were unaware of their entitlements. The super cyclone in Orissa had done a havoc to the poor and it was attributed as a total failure of the state in tackling the disaster. It is understandable that in the absence of clear preparedness naturally the state had to meet with failures.

The Reasons for Government failure in 1999 Super Cyclone are lack of strong State level political leadership, lack of contingency plans, lack of alternative communicative system (the impact of cyclone led to a significant break down of the Orissa Government Infrastructure and communication systems for a period up to two weeks); and lack of detailed warning information to take appropriate preventive actions (the Indian

Meteorology Department (IMD) issued the warning 48 hours before the landfall). But IMD underestimated the severity of the impending storm and notified the administration only about two hours before the breakdown of the communication networks. This situation left very little time for the District Collectors to disseminate the information to the communities.

With regard to NGO-Government Coordination, the government didn't give proper direction to NGOs. The NGOs were very active in the western part of Orissa before 1999 Super Cyclone. The western part of Orissa is mainly poor, less developed and there is a high concentration of tribal people. After the 1999 Super Cyclone, NGOs responded immediately and they had immediate, short term and long term plans. Shortly after the cyclone they engaged mainly in providing emergency food relief, medical and temporary shelters. There was no guidance from the government regarding the relief and rehabilitation efforts. Aid agencies had to decide themselves to what kind of materials to be distributed and which community should have priority? The state's failure to manage relief effectively forced the 40 NGOs to set up the emergency response network called 'The Orissa Disaster Mitigation Mission'.

Each NGOs and INGOs specialized in particular area like housing, gender, community mobilization, distribution of relief, sanitation, agriculture, education, health and carried out activities. The 1999 Super Cyclone provided the impetus for the creation of the OSDMA. Apart from the OSDMA, the Government of Orissa drafted State Disaster Management Plan and a number of community-based disaster management plans. After the 1999 Super Cyclone, Government of Orissa, INGOs, NGOs came together and they devised the mechanism and took innovative measures. They were:

(a) Formation of Orissa State Disaster Mitigation Authority (OSDMA),
(b) Formation of Orissa Disaster Mitigation Mission (ODMM),
(c) Revision of Orissa Relief Code,
(d) Formation of Orissa State Disaster Management Policy,
(e) Implementation of Community-based Disaster Management Plan.

Orissa State Disaster Management Authority

Orissa State Disaster Management Authority (OSDMA) was designed to respond and be prepared. After the 1999 Super Cyclone, OSDMA was established as an exclusive agency for better monitoring of disaster. It was registered under Societies Registration Act. It has rigid financial regulations.

OSDMA was designed to respond and to be prepared to face the disasters, it is a special relief organization and also it concentrates on relief and rehabilitation and reconstruction activities. The mandate of the OSDMA is to increase community resilience, to promote the culture of preparedness towards tropical cyclones and other natural and man-made hazards and to coordinate the activities of the NGOs and other humanitarian organizations, especially, regarding the construction of cyclone centres. This was done through two units. One dealt with social issues of disaster management such as capacity building, disaster preparedness, awareness raising and public education and inter-organizational coordination. And the other is concerned with technocratic approaches to reduce risk and vulnerability, including the construction of cyclone shelters and cyclone resistant houses and infrastructure. It has rigid financial regulation. It works as NGOs but has rigid rules and regulations as government agencies. It also acts as consultant. It regularly gets expertise from civil society organizations. OSDMA and Gujarat State Disaster Mitigation Authority (GSDMA) were the first of their kind in India. OSDMA is headed by the Chief Secretary. But GSDMA is head by the Chief Minister. Like OSDMA and GSDMA, 16 states in India have established their own authority. GSDMA and OSDMA provide institutional framework to deal with disasters. OSDMA has its own distinction, when compared with other state's Disaster Management Authority. OSDMA concentrates on Disaster preparedness. It has GIS cell. If it gets information on disaster, it immediately communicates warning aspects to district officials. It has contract and expand models. During the normal time, 90 per cent of its activities go for preparedness and 10 per cent of its activities go for reconstruction. But if any disaster occurs, 90 per cent of its activities go for reconstruction. By December 2002 the organization had drafted a State Disaster Management Plan and a number of Community-based Disaster Preparedness Plan.

Organization of Disaster Management and Mitigation (ODMM)

Non-Governmental Organizations working for Disaster Management and Mitigation came together and formed a network. They regularly conduct training for Gram Panchayat representatives, formulated Orissa Disaster Management Policy and pressurized Government to bring changes in the Orissa State Relief Code. In the state of Orissa, NGOs are organizing capacity building exercises to the elected representatives of local bodies, NGOs are seeking Panchayat's help to distribute relief materials. With the help of Panchayats, NGOs are making contingency plans.

ODMM is not a relief agency, it is a coordinating agency among NGOs, and Panchayat representatives. At the state level, it acts as a coordinating agency among NGOs, OSDMA and SRC. At the district level, it is trying to maintain proper coordination among district administration and NGOs. It also influences the NGOs to maintain transparency. It also influences the government machineries. In Orissa, the district administration is not serious about conducting coordination meetings regularly. During disaster time, regular meetings are held, but other than that it is not. There should be legal framework or regular coordination meetings, planning and coordination. They should be legalized. In the Orissa relief code, coordination meetings should be held from Panchayat level to the district level. The following should be taken into account for effective disaster management: legality involved, better coordination and synergization, disaster preparedness and community-based management. ODMM conducts capacity building to NGO functionaries, volunteers, and Panchayati Raj Institutions' functionaries. It conducts regular coordination among the state, district and block level officials and representatives, it conducts regular advocacy also.

Revision of Orissa Relief Code

After the 1999 Super Cyclone the Government of Orissa realized the importance of bringing changes in its policy and practice and brought the following changes in the Orissa Relief Code:

(a) Scope and provision of relief with a vulnerability focus;
(b) Entitlements of the victims of the calamity;
(c) Assessment of the damage and the timeline;
(d) Role of Panchayati Raj Institutions in disaster preparedness and response;
(e) Devolutions of powers to PRIs to ensure the effective emergency response;

(f) Scope of assessment of damage to livelihood options to be broadened;
(g) Focus on rehabilitation, reconstruction and mitigation;
(h) Immediate development of disaster management plans including hazard and vulnerability mapping, with enhanced community participation at all levels of community Panchayat, block and district;
(i) Strengthening of district control rooms and development of standard operating procedures at every level which takes effect immediately and after red alert is sounded or red alert is declared;
(j) Community-based drainage plans combined with scientific inputs with emphasis on local ownership or management of the flood control structures;
(k) Inter-district and inter-state response plans need to be developed by each district and coordinated by SRC/OSDMA;
(l) Decentralized stock pilings for essential communication, evacuation, search, rescue and relief items with a web-based inventory tracking system;
(m) Need for regular updating of disaster management plans and also mock drills for intra and inter-district response;
(n) Provision for rewarding officials displaying risk-taking abilities and commitments;
(o) Building an agenda of community health care;
(p) Providing perspectives solutions for long term disaster; and
(q) As for as NGOs are concerned they formed Flood Management Committees at the village level and they made Panchayat representatives as members of the committee. NGOs activities were implemented through this committee.

With regard to damage assessment, the district followed the relief code norms for damage assessment. While the damage to public properties was dealt with by the respective departments promptly, house damage, crop and land loss assessments were undertaken quite late (according to the perception of the community). There were practical difficulties in assessing house damages and sand cast on cultivable land. The time lag in damage assessment adversely affected the rehabilitation plans in many cases discouraging the community from undertaking any restoration work till the revenue authorities inspected the affected area to assess damaged properties. Local community-based organizations or the Gram Panchayats did not have any role in damage assessment. The community was dissatisfied with the process of damage assessment mainly due to the lack of transparency. The assessment of damage cost to the community mental health and personal belongings remained uncertain.

Disaster Management Policy

In the state of Orissa, disasters are regular phenomena. By considering this the Revenue Department has been renamed as Revenue and Disaster Management Department as per the notification of the Government *vide* No. 12355/SER 11, dated 5-6-2006. In the context of proclamation of International Decade for Natural Disaster Reduction (IDNDR); the state government felt it necessary to have a specific policy for Disaster Management and to provide necessary guidelines on all aspects of emergency management. Hence, the Government had evolved a policy. The government of Orissa Disaster Management Policy was on total risk management and vulnerability reduction by strengthening the physical infrastructure as well as bio, physical, psychological, social and economic status of the people and to make the people have increasing.

Principles of the Disaster Management Policy

Following are the key principles of the policy:

(a) Take a proactive approach to disaster management and promote a culture of prevention and preparedness among individuals and institutions;
(b) Follow a multi-hazard approach to disaster management;
(c) Shift from a relief and welfare approach to a rights and entitlement-based approach to humanitarian assistance;
(d) Since sustainable development will not be possible without the active involvement of the communities, make the vulnerability reduction programmes community-driven;
(e) Integrate Disaster Management into Development Policy and Planning;
(f) Institutionalize efficient, well-coordinated and participatory disaster management initiatives as one of the basic ingredients of good governance;
(g) Ensure quality at all stages of emergency management including prevention, mitigation, relief and reconstruction and make their

adoption mandatory. For doing so, universally accepted minimum standards will be adopted. If necessary, the standards would be modified taking into account the local conditions and customs;

(h) Attempt harmonious blending of all disaster management interventions with local cultural ethos;

(i) Focus on protection of the environment;

(j) Promote inter-agency coordination and cooperation for Disaster Management;

(k) Involve all stake holders in disaster management and define their roles in different stages of disasters;

(l) Create an enabling environment for ensuring higher participation of all stakeholders;

(m) Work on legislation(s) to provide statutory backing to essential disaster management functions and agencies;

(n) Establish a trigger mechanism for emergency operations;

(o) View people as valuable partners and strengthen community-based coping mechanisms for dealing with disasters;

(p) Promote a spirit of volunteerism, develop a cadre of well-trained volunteers whose services will be utilized during emergencies;

(q) Document and use people's indigenous knowledge, whenever possible;

(r) Share information and knowledge about disasters and their management with all stakeholders;

(s) Develop a network amongst various disaster management entities using OSDMA as the main hub;

(t) Establish an Institute dedicated to conducting research, development and training on disaster management related activities;

(u) Make Disaster Management a part of the educational system and curricula;

(v) Decentralized management of disasters to the Block, Gram Panchayat/Municipality levels and strengthen their institutional and functional capacities to be effective as the first responders to disaster events;

(w) Ensure that humanitarian assistance is provided in an equitable, consistent and predictable manner;

(x) Emphasize participation of women in all stages of Disaster management and recognize their special problems in disaster situations; and

(y) Recognize the higher vulnerability of children, elders, physically and mentally challenged, during and after emergencies and design interventions accordingly.

Strategy

Disaster management will have an integrated approach covering three phases of disasters, namely:

(a) Pre-disasters,
(b) Response, and
(c) Recovery and rehabilitation.

Revenue department is the nodal department for disaster management. OSDMA is the coordinating agency in pre-disaster and post-disaster phass. It is the special relief organization and it leads during the response phase. District Collectors and their officers are the nodal agencies at district level for prevention, response and recovery in the event of all types of disasters. Integrating Disaster Management with development planning is very important and hence, relevant departments have to earmark certain portions of the plan budgets to undertake prevention measures.

For capacity building of the elected representatives of officials Civil Society Organization are important. Constitution of specialized task force has to be done. Ensuring committee participation is more important at the synergization of activities of the NGOs, CBOs, and other civil society institutions are essential for effective disaster management. Community system has to be strengthened. Inventory of resources, both human and material has to be identified, and documented at the village level. Assessing the shelter needs is more important with the participation of the community. Strengthening of infrastructure is yet another prime activity. Environmental protection is an imperative. Including disaster management in educational curriculum is more important for creating a preparedness culture among the people. Promoting effective and comprehensive insurance coverage is also important. According to the government of Orissa State Disaster Management Policy, OSDMA will revise and update the policy as and when required.

Monitoring Committees

Cabinet or Cabinet sub-committee will take stock of the situation during disaster. The official committee will be headed by the Chief Secretary. A Special Relief Commission will be there to monitor relief, rehabilitation, and reconstruction process during and after disaster. A District Collector will lead the team at the district level. Rapid damage assessment will be done by the district administration and concerned departments.

Resource Mobilization

According to Orissa Disaster Management Policy, assistance will be sought from union government, public, private sector, multi-lateral and bi-lateral agencies, UN organizations, the civil societies and other charitable organizations. OSDMA will document the various aspects of disaster management regularly.

Community-based Disaster Preparedness

It is a response mechanism to save life, livelihood, livestock and assets with available resources. It leads to multi-pronged development interventions to address the root causes of vulnerability. It leads to a self-reliant disaster proof community.

Components of Community-based Disaster Preparedness

Following are the components:

(a) Zoning of the areas;
(b) Networking among CBOs/NGOs/Civil Societies response groups;
(c) Training of block/GP/CBOs on disaster management and implementation strategy;
(d) Facilitate implementation process by CBOs/GP/Block/District;
(e) Identification of volunteers from each village;
(f) Training of volunteers of Community Contingency Plan (CCP) developments;
(g) CCP development at village level;
(h) Formation of task forces; and
(i) Mock drills.

Approach

Community-based disaster preparedness has the following approaches:

(a) Sensitization/Awareness;
(b) Review and analysis;
(c) Situational analysis;
(d) Hazard mapping;
(e) Risk mapping; and
(f) Opportunity mapping.

Stages of Community Contingency Plan Preparation

Table 2.1 gives the details of steps to be followed to prepare a community contingency plan with the active participation of stakeholders.

Sustainability of Community-based Approaches

To institutionalize the process the contingency plan has to be approved by the Palli Sabha and village assembly. Emergency fund has to be generated. Regular capacity building of task force is to be conducted. Regular support for the task force members by the NGOs, INGOs and government have to be extended. Linkages with other institutions have to established.

Mitigation Strategy: Risk Reduction

There are different steps taken by the Government through a well-planned strategy. There are:

1. Safe shelter;
2. Elevated land;
3. Insurance;
4. Retrofitting the traditional structure;
5. Alternative cropping pattern;
6. Short duration crop;
7. Grain or seed bank;
8. Accurate and timely warning;
9. Identification and registration of risk groups; and
10. Integrating development programmes to reduce vulnerability.

Tamil Nadu

In Tamil Nadu, Disaster is a regular phenomenon. Apart from 2004 tsunami cyclone, flood and landslides regularly hit Tamil Nadu. In the

Table 2.1: Steps to be Followed for Preparing Contingency Plan

1.	Review Analysis of Past Disasters	Learning from past disasters: before, during and after in terms of warning, relief and rehabilitation
2.	Situational Analysis	Topographic features and Demographic details: house, land, field, forest, water bodies and infrastructures
3.	Hazard Factors	Location and Causes of hazards: To find out the direction of winds, water flow, land slides
4.	Vulnerability Assessment	High Risk Group: Elderly and disabled, children, sick, single woman etc. Property: Livestock, livelihood and assets, water sources
5.	Resource Identification	Existing Resources: Safe Shelter, natural barrier, safe water, sanitation facility, food/grain stock, warehouses, health services, communication facilities etc.
6.	Formation of Task Force	Community Task forces for: warning, rescue and evacuation, water and sanitation, relief and food, damage assessment, first aid, shelter etc.
7.	Capacity Building of Task Force	Training of Task forces: On Health and first aid, water and sanitation, rescue, warning to carryout their responsibility effectively.
8.	Contingency Fund	Fund to meet emergency needs: Contribution for stock piling of food, medicine, equipments, and emergency needs for lives and livestock.
9.	Preparedness and Drill	Practice of plan: Task force members practice the plan periodically before possible disaster season.

Source: Computed.

year 1883, on 26th August, an explosion of the Krokatoa Volcano in Indonesia caused the tsunami in East Coast of India. 2m tsunamis were recorded at Chennai. Again an 8.1 Richter scale earthquake in Andaman Archipelago. In the year 1941, on 26th June also affected East Coast of India. But no estimate of the height of the tsunami is available. In the year 1977 cyclone hit Chennai, Kerala and Andhra Pradesh. The estimated death toll to the cyclone is 14,204 (*source*, Office of the US Foreign

Assistance). Again in the year 1984 cyclone hit Tamil Nadu and Andhra Pradesh and destroyed 512 precious lives.

With respect to landslides in the 1919 October, Nilgris was affected. It led to the killing of 36 people. Several people were injured, several buildings and communication network were damaged. Again in the year 1992 in the month of November landslides occurred in Nilgris. Due to this road network and buildings were damaged. The total damage was estimated at Rs. 5 million. In the year 1993, landslides happened in Nilgris which led to the killing of 40 people and property worth several lakhs was damaged.

In above all the disasters, the Government of Tamil Nadu responded promptly and quickly. But it didn't establish permanent structure to respond to the disasters. Like that in the year 2004, the tsunami struck Tamil Nadu, the waves measured around 10 m height and killing more than 10,000 people in the coastal districts of Tamil Nadu. Like previous experience the Government of Tamil Nadu took positive measures and the prompt action was coordinated between the Government Departments and the non-government organizations in relief operations. The Government of Tamil Nadu has developed a clear-cut perspective and accordingly it carried out relief activities.

The Government Orders were issued immediately after tsunami struck on the (a) release of Chief Minister's public relief fund (G.O. MS No. 574 dated 28-12-2004), (b) relief package assistance sanctioned from Calamity Relief Fund (G.O. MS No. 575, dated 28-12-2004) (c) distribution of temporary ration cards (G.O. MS No. 380, dated 31-12-2004).

It also issued more than 130 Government Orders. It also constituted an empowered committee for monitoring the proper implementation of the schemes under the Prime Ministers' National Fund with an officer on Special duty (relief and rehabilitation) to coordinate, review and monitor the activities. The empowered committee guided the officer on special duty. At the district level immediately after the tsunami struck, the district administration prioritized the activities and acted accordingly. The district administration carried out the activities in the following order:

(a) Rescue of survivors;
(b) Removal and disposal of dead bodies;
(c) Setting up of relief centres;
(d) Providing temporary shelters and food to the affected families;

(e) Restoration of electricity, water supply etc.;
(f) Maintaining sanitation; and
(g) Prevention of epidemic.

To meet the challenge of reaching out to everyone of the affected habitations, Government of Tamil Nadu formed eleven self-contained area teams to cover six to seven continuous habitations. Each team was supervised by a Minster or Board Chairman with one IAS officer as the team leader. Each team leader (IAS Officer) was given Rs. 5 lakhs in cash and the financial freedom to take decisions on the spot regarding expenditure. Along with Revenue Department officials, Rural Development Department officials headed by the Rural Development and Panchayati Raj Secretary were involved in relief operations.

The team had proper coordination with district administration. The District Revenue Officer was appointed at the headquarters to handle logistics. Apart from that daily press briefing, all the team leaders sat together every night to share their experiences and to get proper direction from their colleagues. This gave them proper coordination.

Apart from that Government of Tamil Nadu had established proper coordination mechanism to receive and distribute relief materials. The other Government departments like, Tamil Nadu Electricity Board, Tamil Nadu State Transport Corporation, Tamil Nadu Civil Supply Corporation, Tamil Nadu Water Supply and Drainage Board, Forest and Animal Husbandry Department did commendable work in receiving relief material and distributing them.

Unlike in Orissa the Government of Tamil Nadu and NGOs had proper coordination to distribute the relief materials. The INGOs and the NGOs have ten-day, three-month, six-month and three-year plans. Most of the INGOs and the NGOs had only three-year plan for the disaster related works. It also happened in Tamil Nadu.

The international organizations and the non-governmental organizations were working with the following principles with regard to disaster:

1. *People Centred*: Most of the organizations worked with pro-poor disadvantaged and marginalized approach.
2. *Participation*: Organizations were committed to ensure the local people's participation and stakeholder's involvement in all their

projects. They were also committed for the strengthening of the local institutions and action on the basis of help for self help.

3. *Development Oriented*: Many of them declared that the activities should have focus with development.
4. *Gender Sensitivity*: Organization made it very clear that all the relief and rehabilitation activities should be carried out with a gender perspective. A gender sensitize approach should be infused in every action.
5. *Sustainability*: Sustainability is seen as a core principle.

A coordination committee was formed to interface between the NGOs and Government on the activities to be carried out in the affected areas. However, it was also observed that some of the non-governmental organizations had been kept out of coordination with others. While their reluctance to share information with others was a major factor, these organizations doubted the behind the scene motivation as the reason for keeping out of coordination. There might have been lurking fear over the coordination cell that it would assume authority to control over them and it would work as a mouth piece of the Government.

It has been found that several of the non-governmental organizations involved in tsunami operations did not have much consultation of the leaders of the local communities. As a result, these organizations remained unaware of the historical, social and economic conditions that had prevailed in the tsunami-affected costal regions (such as the culture of sharing everything equally within the community, the role of traditional fishing panchayats). Consequently, the relief provided among such communities was leading to social conflict, and the affected communities could now be worse off with relief than before. Similarly, the study found that many of the non-governmental organizations had as part of the relief efforts adopted smaller villages with less population and some of the larger villages were left out. As relief has poured into the smaller villages the distribution of relief was unequal leading to discord among the villagers.

Another major drawback in the relief efforts by the state and the non-state agencies has been the gross negligence of the plight of the farmers who lived further inland in Tamil Nadu and had been affected by the tsunami. During Tsunami the sea water carried by the massive waves seeped into farm lands destroyed standing crops, left behind a lot of silt and turned the soil into the saline waste. According to many farmers in Nagapattinam district in Tamil Nadu, it could take up to five years or more to desalinate their lands. However, their problems were almost completely ignored by the relief providing agencies in the state in the first phase of the relief.

Box 1
Distribution of Relief Materials

In Prathaba Rama Puram Panchayat NGOs and Government distributed more relief materials than required. For example. one NGO distributed water packets. Immediately after half an hour another NGO distributed water bottles. So these people threw away the water packets and started collecting the water bottles. Like that the Government of Tamil Nadu distributed cooked rice packets (Sambar Rice). Each person got 10 to 12 food packets at a time. The next day everybody started throwing the remaining food packets. Like that in the beginning affected people accepted old dresses. Once they started getting new ones they started throwing away old one. Managing the waste became a problem for the Gram Panchayats.

But most of the organizations did not have faith in local body institutions. Many of the organizations lack disaster perspective and as a result October to December 2005 saw persistent heavy rains which cost severe flooding in fifteen districts of Tamil Nadu. While loss of life was minimal when compared to tsunami, but the media coverage was poor, the flooding affected twenty times more than the population affected by the tsunami the previous year and the community suffered huge losses but all international organizations and non-governmental organizations did not realize this impact. Finally, when people were contacted, it was the unanimous response that neither communities nor the Panchayats were consulted in taking major decisions. As a result people suffered during the floods.

Andhra Pradesh

Andhra Pradesh is no different from other Indian states with regard to disaster. On 19th November, 1977, cyclone and tidal waves killed 20,000 people. In the year 1989 death toll due to flood was 1591, again in the year 1997, 1442 people were killed in Andhra Pradesh. In the year 2000, 1290 people were killed due to flood. In the year 1972, cyclone took away 100 precious lives. Again, in the year 1977, cyclone hit the coasts of Chennai, Kerala and Andhra Pradesh and 14,204 people lost their lives. In the years 1979, 1984, 1985 and 1990 the following death tolls were recorded, 594, 512, 5000 and 957.

In the year 2004 tsunami struck the coastal Andhra Pradesh. Floods in major rivers are a regular phenomenon. The flood causes extensive loss of human lives, cattle, property and the public life comes to a stand still for the periods ranging from ten to twenty years. The behavioural attitude of the Godavari river is not uniform and similar in all the floods that occurred in the past. In the district of Nellore inlet and outlet channels (like Cauvery delta) major ponds and tanks were not desilted properly. Many of the tank areas became housing colonies. This created a major flood in Nellore district. The devastating cyclones and floods in Andhra Pradesh prompted the Government to strengthen their infrastructures. In this regard the Government of Andhra Pradesh for example constructed more than 1000 cyclone shelters after the cyclone in 1977 killed some 10,000 people. Apart from that it prepared Godavari Flood Scheme in the year 1984. The flood manual was regularly updated thereafter. In the flood manual Government of Andhra Pradesh established well structured organizational setup to tackle flood disaster.

Organizational Setup

Advisory Setup

Three levels of structures are working in the advisory setup, i.e. State level, District level and Divisional level. It has been mentioned in the Godavari Flood Manual.

Executive Setup

Sectoral Officers

There are nine sectors in the Godavari Delta area and for each sector, sectorwise officers have been appointed. TA Officer in the cadre of Deputy Collector or Senior District Officer will be the Sectoral Officer, who is responsible both for evacuation and relief operations.

Zonal Officers

The Zonal officers will be appointed to help the village teams under the respective jurisdiction and they will be guided and coordinated by the

Sectoral Officer. The main duties of the Zonal Officers are that they are coordinating officers between the Sectoral Officers, mobile officers and village teams.

Village Teams

Village Teams work under the supervision and guidance of sectoral officers. For evacuation and relief operations during the menace, the village teams are constituted with the following members: (i) Local Teacher; (ii) Local VDO; (iii) Local VAO; (iv) Village Sarpanch or Village Elder (Non-Official).

Mobile Team

The Mobile teams have been constituted for proper monitoring, communication and rescue and relief operations during the actual disaster situation. The team consists of one Mobile Officer, one Member of GCC, one member from Medical and Health Department and 2 to 3 police constables.

Warning and Communication Systems

Warning System

In Khammam district, Andhra Pradesh warning will be given at three levels.

First Warning Level (Precautionary Stage)

First warning will be issued when the flood level reaches to 43 ft or 16.11 m. in the scale kept by Central Water Commission at Bhadrachalam, through Radio Message.

Second Warning Level (Action Stage)

Second warning will be issued when the flood level reaches 48 ft at Bhadrachalam, through the Radio Message.

Third Warning Level (Evacuation Stage)

Third warning will be issued when the flood level reaches 53 ft in Bhadrachalam, through the Radio Message.

Communication System

The main communication system at all the time is the telephone but during the flood the telephone system will also be dead and so the Khammam district administration has invented the following communication systems:

(a) Revenue Motorola sets;
(b) Police Motorola Wireless sets;
(c) HAM sets;
(d) Radio Sets; and
(d) Telephones.

Control Rooms

The control rooms have been set up at village, block and at district level. All these control rooms will function round the clock and the officer in charge will prepare a duty chart keeping two persons at a time for duty for every six hours. During the time of turbulence, every duty officer/ staff member should be authorized to handle all flood messages over police VHF and Hamsets according to the necessity.

Pre-Flood Preparatory Stage

There are some pre-floods preparatory which are well laid in the Godavari Flood Manual. They are:

Trainings: The mobile team at the village level will be trained in the disaster management activities such as rescue and relief.

Civil Supplies Preparedness: In order to ensure that essential commodities are available during the flood season a meeting has to be conducted at District Level by the District Collector with the flood-prone area Mandal Revenue Officers, GCC staff and Divisional Officers every year in the month of May and it has to be ensured that stocks reach the identified places by the end of June every year.

Buffer Stocks: Buffer stock is the stock of rice and kerosene oil kept at certain identified places in the mandals which has to be used in eventuality of occurrence of floods. Besides, the buffer stock sufficient quantity of food grains and other essential commodities like sugar, kerosene should be available in the flood affected villages for the sale to the local population during flood season since some of the villages will be encircled by flood water and will remain isolated for quite some time.

Vehicles: The Sub Collector should also ensure that all the government vehicles being requisitioned for flood duty are kept road-worthy by the respective departments.

Minimum Bank Balance: The Sub Collector should also ensure that the SBH Branches of the district should keep a minimum bank balance of Rs. 50.00 lakhs each during the flood season, i.e. July to September. Godavari water level increases gradually, MRO instructs and inform village servants regarding flood level.

Government totally depends on the village revenue officer. He is the lowest rank servant in the revenue department. Committees are there at Mandal and Zilla Panchayat level. But committee comprises only the officials. If flood warning is given, they appoint government teachers or any other government servants. They have to stay in the village, till flood recedes. Gram Panchayat does not have exact data and they do not have disaster preparedness plan.

The District Collectors are requested to conduct flood management meetings twice a year. Loss of Lives and Properties in Tsunami 2004: The official toll is 105. The affected districts are Krishna (35 dead), Prakasam (35 dead), Nellore (20 dead), Guntur (4 dead), West Godavari (8 dead) and East Godavari (3 dead).

People affected by the Tsunami disaster were 196,000 in Andhra Pradesh. The tsunami destroyed over 235,000 homes, damaged 83,788 boats and rendered 39,035 hectares of cropped area unusable. The social infrastructure—schools, primary health centres, drinking water supply, anganwadis and other community assets—in these areas were totally destroyed. The total cost of damages was Rs. 3.42 billion in Andhra Pradesh. In the state-wise break up of the package was: Andhra Pradesh was provided Rs. 7 million. Second, in the Planning Commission, the government set up a Core Group on Reconstruction, Management and Monitoring for tsunami affected areas. The Core Group prepared a comprehensive plan for rehabilitation and reconstruction of the affected states, with a financial outlay of Rs. 1.38 billion for Andhra Pradesh.

As far as NGOs and INGOs are concerned in Andhra Pradesh, they work separately and they don't have coordination among themselves. A few NGOs closely worked with District Administration for the distribution of relief materials. They too worked at village level and they did not have faith in local body institutions. Relief materials were distributed through committees formed by them. All NGOs work with Gender sensitized way and they follow equity. There are many parallel structures in the Andhra Pradesh villages. NGOs regularly provide relief materials after any disaster. Each NGO has specialized in a particular area and they are concentrating on that. The NGOs don't concentrate on rehabilitation and reconstruction activities. The NGOs are selecting a few villages and concentrating on them and the other villages were neglected both by the NGOs and the Government.

Gujarat

In the State of Gujarat, 1994 flood killed 2000 people and affected thousands. Apart from that flood occurred in 1980, 1989, 1997 and 2000 killed thousands of people. In the 1960s, an earthquake hit in Anjar with the magnitude of 7.0 Richter scale. In the year 2001 another earthquake occurred in Bhuj with the magnitude of 6.9 Richter scale. The seismic zoning map of India showed that the Gujarat has very high risk quakes of magnitude 8 and greater. Apart from that cyclone occurred in Gujarat in the year 1981 and in 1982 with the loss of life about 470 and 500 respectively. Like other states of India, Government of Gujarat also was not much concentrated on disaster preparedness before Bhuj and Kutch earthquake. Even though Gujarat is placed under high risk zone, many of the buildings didn't follow the rules regarding construction. After the Kutch and Bhuj earthquake, Government of Gujarat and Non-Government Organizations, took a number of measures. With regard to Government of Gujarat the entire State machinery was mobilized to do relief and rehabilitation work. Once relief phase is over the Government of Gujarat formulated the disaster management policy and formed a separate structure called Gujarat State Disaster Management Authority.

The state of Gujarat has been prone to disaster such as cyclones, droughts, floods and earthquake which caused extensive damage to life and property and had impact on its economic development. In response to this, the Government of Gujarat decided to formulate a policy which enshrines various aspects of management to deal with disasters in systematic and sustainable manner.

In order to achieve its objective of institutionalizing a disaster management framework in the state, the Government of Gujarat (GoG) has established a nodal agency named Gujarat State Disaster Management Authority to facilitate, coordinate and monitor disaster management activities and promote reasonable disaster management and mitigation practices in the state. The establishment of GSDMA is a key element in the overall disaster management policy of the state government.

Gujarat State Disaster Management Authority

The GSDMA was constituted by the Government of Gujarat by GAD's resolution dated 8th February, 2001. This authority has been created as a permanent arrangement to handle natural calamities. The objectives for the constitution of this authority have been clearly spelt out in the document.

These are,

(a) To provide relief to the people for the loss incurred due to natural calamity and to undertake rehabilitation and reconstruction as also social and economic activities or restoration of the situation;
(b) To make efforts to minimize the impact of natural calamities through precautionary programmes and schemes;
(c) To analyse and study the reasons of natural calamities; and
(d) The headquarters of this authority (GSDMA) was established in Gandhinagar and its jurisdiction was throughout the entire state of Gujarat. It was supposed to function as an autonomous body.

Activities

Its activities are non-profitable and was registered as a charitable institution under the Societies Registration Act, 1980 with the competent authorities. The authorities were working under the aegis of the Rehabilitation and Reconstruction Division as a separate cell created under GAD. In the year 2002, the Government of Gujarat declared 'Disaster Management Policy' for the State. Following this policy the government passed 'Gujarat State Disaster Management Act, 2003'. The bill was passed by the state assembly on March 28, 2003 and the Act came into force from May 13, 2003. With this, the state of Gujarat was the first state in India to have enacted the Act to provide legal and regulatory framework for disaster management.

With the effect of Gujarat State Disaster Management Act, 2003, the society which was constituted earlier as GSDMA was dissolved under section 49 of the Act and the authority under Sub-section 1 of the Section 6 came to an existence. Thus the Government of Gujarat *vide* Notification No. DMA-1003-1488-B, dated 29th August, 2003 in the Official Gazette established an authority in the name of Gujarat State Disaster Management Authority with effect from 1st September, 2003 and specified Gandhi Nagar as the headquarters of the said authority under the sub-sections (1) and (3) of the Section 6 of the Act.

Constitution of the Authority

Under the Section 7 of the GSDM Act 2003 provides the constitution of authority.

Appointment of the Members

The GSDMA shall consists of Chairperson and not more than fourteen members. They are:

(a) Chief Minister of the state, who shall be the ex-officio chairperson;
(b) Two ministers nominated by the Chief Minister by virtue of their office amongst the council of ministers of the state;
(c) The Chief Secretary of the State, ex-officio;
(d) The Secretary to the Government of Gujarat, Revenue Department, ex-officio;
(e) The Chief Executive Officer of the Authority, ex-officio;
(f) The State Relief Commissioner, ex-officio;
(g) The Director General of Police of the State, ex-officio; and
(h) Such other officers of the state government as may be appointment by the state government by virtue of their office.

When a proclamation made under Article 356 of the Constitution is in force in the State which states that the Central Government may appoint three persons, in place of the Chief Minister and other two ministers to be the Chairperson and member of the Authority and the persons so appointed shall vacate their office upon the revocation of operation of such a proclamation.

Office Duration for the Authorities

The members of the Authority shall hold office during the presence of the state government and receive remuneration as may be prescribed.

Aim of the GSDMA

To go beyond reconstruction and make Gujarat economically vibrant, agriculturally and industrially competitive with improved standards of living with a capacity to mitigate and manage future disasters.

The entire nation rallied to share the grief of the people of Gujarat and relief and support poured in from all over the world. The government understood the need for the addressing the issue of long term rehabilitation with the support of external development agencies. The government prepared Gujarat Earthquake Rehabilitation and Reconstruction Policy with the aim of making it a people's programme. On the advice of the government, the NGOs played a key role in rehabilitation activities. These NGOs were allocated the villages with more than 50 per cent of the destruction. Abhiyan was reported to be one of the leading network of NGOs which played a major role in coordinating various technical experts like physicians, engineers, social workers, counsellors, etc.

The Gujarat State Disaster Management Authority framed some guidelines. They are:

(a) To involve people and representatives institutions in the decision making process and reflect the priorities and aspirations in programme deliverables;
(b) To strengthen civil society institutions like NGOs, community based organizations and women groups in the implementation process;
(c) Equity and empowerment assured through appropriate mechanisms that the voices of the weak and the poor are always heard;
(d) Beneficiaries and the stakeholders—choice regarding construction; and
(e) Ensure highest level of transparency and accountability in the programme implementation through appropriate institutional mechanisms and practices.

Implementation Strategy

It is a carefully devised strategy, which harmonises the emergency nature of reconstruction programme with a strong emphasis on community participation and seismic safety measures. The main elements of the implementation strategies were:

(a) Carry out an in-depth damage assessment;
(b) Conduct a social impact assessment;
(c) Set up a public-private participation;
(d) Encouraged owner-driven and hazard resistant construction;
(e) Establish community participation mechanism and facilitate decision making at the community level;
(f) Disseminate information about the rehabilitation programme and people's entitlements; and
(g) Emphasize social and community development and gender empowerment.

The Gujarat State Disaster Management Policy consists of three phases and they are:

(i) Pre-disaster phase;
(ii) Disaster/Impact phase; and
(iii) Post-disaster phase.

The order to carry out the activities in the three phases, Government of Gujarat has formulated a framework with a set of agencies such as:

(a) Gujarat State Disaster Management Authority;
(b) State Relief Commissioner;
(c) Government Departments;
(d) District Administration, headed by the District Collector;
(e) Local Authorities, including Municipal Corporations, Districts, Taluks, Gram Panchayats etc.;
(f) Voluntary agencies, including NGO;
(g) Public sector;
(h) Private sector; and
(i) Important role by community.

The Pre-disaster phase includes prevention, mitigation and preparedness activities. These activities involve extensive data collection, maintaining directories of resources, developing action plans, capacity building, training and community awareness activities, among others. Government departments, district administration local authorities and other relevant agencies will develop plans for prevention and mitigation of disasters and will built capacity and ensure preparedness in the event of a disaster actually taking place.

But still now many villages even in Gujarat and other disaster-prone districts, steps have not been taken regarding planning, preparing data collection and maintaining directories of resources, suppose any village panchayat maintained full data of the village, it would avoid duplication or flow of excess resources to the village in disaster time, for example, in Tamil Nadu, during Tsunami time a lot of resources were wasted in many place in the absence of such data at panchayat level.

The Gujarat State Disaster Management Policy has mentioned some key activities in pre-disaster phase such as

(i) Planned development;
(ii) Development of policies and guidelines;
(iii) Establishing a proper chain of command;
(iv) Risk assessment;
(v) Develop disaster management plans;
(vi) Develop responsibilities of information;
(vii) Establish communication and technology network;
(viii) Developing early warning mechanisms;
(ix) Establish flexible procedure;
(x) Building capabilities and expertise;
(xi) Capacity building;
(xii) Health and medical care;
(xiii) Knowledge management;
(xiv) Funds generation; and
(xv) Identifying avenues for risk sharing and transferring.

Even though it is clearly mentioned in the policy, that developing early warning mechanisms, except for a very few villages, many villages and many people even have not heard about that concept. Likewise, the other states also have not got the experience from Gujarat. For example, in Gujarat State Disaster Management Policy, it is mentioned that risk assessment as main activities, if it was done carefully, many lives may be saved. In Tamil Nadu, Samiyarpettai Village Panchayat, Parangipettai Block, Cuddalore District and Leepuram Village Panchayat of Kanyakumari District had undergone the Disaster Management Training, so that the loss of lives was low when compared to the neighbouring villages.

Another key activity is capacity building among the communities in the concept of Disaster Management. For this, the GSDMA had formed a committee named Disaster Management Committee and also gave one or two training sessions which was not sufficient because many people were unable to remember the committee's name. But, AIDMI now is playing a predominate role in Building Capacity among the people. Funds generation is one of the vital activities of pre-disaster phase and policy states that, Government of Gujarat intends to have a budgetary allocation for disaster management and funds would be made available through the Calamity Relief Fund. But in no village there is separate account for Disaster Management.

Gujarat State Disaster Management Act

Gujarat Act No. 20 of 2003—provides for effective management of disaster for mitigation of the effects of disaster for administering, facilitating, coordinating and monitoring emergency relief during and after the occurrence of disaster and for implementing, monitoring and coordinating measures in the state of Gujarat. In this regard the main powers and functions of the collector and local authorities are mentioned in Chapters IX and X of the Act under Clauses 23, 24 and 25, of these the main function, towards local government by the collector are as follows:

1. Collector shall facilitate and coordinate with local government bodies to ensure that pre-disaster and disaster management activities in the district are carried out;
2. Facilitate community training, awareness programmes and installation of emergency facilities with the support of local administration, non-governmental organization and private sector; and
3. Ensure that local authorities in the district are involved in developing their own mitigation strategies.

Impact of Phase—Emergency Relief Measures and Relief

This is the second phase, the major activities of this phase is clearly listed out as search and rescue, subsistence, shelter, health, sanitation, infrastructure, essential services, security, communication, preliminary damage assessment, funds generation, finalizing relief payouts and packages, post-relief assessment. In this phase, the government, NGOs and Religious organizations carried out many of the activities, despite unforgettable extensive works carried out by panchayats and communities, in many decision making process they had been ignored.

The third phase is post-disaster phase, the main activities are reconstruction and rehabilitation. The thrust of Government policy in this phase will be to ensure a speedy return to normalcy and mitigation of long-term consequences of the disaster. The Gujarat State is in this phase. Not only government but also, NGOs and INGOs have been contributing magnificently. It is difficult to analyse this phase because it is still in process.

The Gujarat earthquake rehabilitation and reconstruction project comprises a number of components like housing, livelihood support programme, infrastructure, social and community development and disaster management. While constructing the houses the government had assessed the damage with people's participation and classified them into five categories as G1, G2, G3, G4, G5.

NGOs Perception

As far as NGOs are concerned they concentrate on relief in the beginning. Once the relief phase is over the NGOs work closely with community in Disaster Preparedness and Management. Many innovative measures were taken by NGOs which were replicated when tsunami struck in Tamil Nadu.

1. Formation of Network among NGOs.
2. Implementing sustainable activities.
3. Motivating experts to join the network to do the relief activities.

Motivated and trained the constitutional Panchayat itself in disaster preparedness and management instead of forming a separate committee for disaster. NGOs issued cards to each household in order to avoid duplication. As per the guidelines of GSDMA the NGOs have to involve and active participation of the communities. Also the NGOs helped the communities in getting relief materials if they found any difficulties in getting them. Some NGOs, instead of providing relief materials involved in long sustainable recovery of the communities from disaster.

Box 2
Network Formation with different NGOs

An NGO named Abhiyan, which is a network of 30 non-governmental organization spread across Kutch. This network emerged as a response to the 1998 Kandla Cyclone where it became a coordinating point between NGOs, a forum for advocacy and policy recommendation to the government, a platform for collective implementation and a facilitator between affected communities, donors, NGOs and government. It has been involved predominantly in disaster management in Kutch which has seen two cyclones, three droughts and an earthquake. This concept was also accepted by Aga Khan Foundation and they said that "we (different professional organizations) worked under one roof and had different experiences which we never had before. This helped us to gain more knowledge in different subjects and we were able to fulfil the lacuna in the beginning state itself. This type of network formation experience helped in Nagapattinam in Tamil Nadu to work without wastage of resources at the time of disaster.

Reduced Duplication of Work in Relief Activities

The NGO, named Aga Khan Foundation, working in various villages for relief work issued token cards in different colours to every household to collect relief activities. The system of issuing cards reduced duplication of work in relief activities. And the strategy of issuing different colour card ensured the equity principle among the communities and also transparency was maintained.

To sum up, disasters have been occurring regularly in the four states, but Government of Tamil Nadu and Andhra Pradesh didn't have comprehensive disaster management policy at the state level like Gujarat and Orissa. Government of Orissa learnt lessons from the 1999 Super Cyclone and took many innovative steps to mitigate disaster. NGOs are cooperating with Government of Orissa in implementing community based disaster management programme. Even though it had a few grey areas that are to be addressed immediately. They are:

1. Programmes are to be institutionalised;
2. Not much importance given to local body institutions except a few NGOs;
3. District collectors are not conducting disaster management meetings regularly;

Box 3

A Different thinking by one NGO to Relieve the Community from Mental Stress

Some of the NGOs like AIDMI and Aga Khan Foundation worked towards long term and sustainable work such as construction of check dams and dealing with micro insurance schemes. During earthquake, in one of the villages a dam was fully damaged. By seeing this, people were mentally disturbed and were not getting regular sleep. After 20 days, the NGO Aga Khan Foundation got the news, and they took the initiative and started working, because they had to complete the work before June, otherwise work might not proceed due to the arrival of monsoon season. Due to less time, getting labourers from outside was difficult, so village people were involved in constructing the dam. This shows that people who were affected mentally were involved with 'Cash for Work' which was a short term relief support given to the community to come out from the trauma through job opportunity.

4. There was lack of continuous training for community and local body leaders; and
5. Lack of exclusive capacity building exercise to the Gram panchayat presidents. They lack sensitivity on the importance of local body institutions, powers, functions and functionaries.

As far as Tamil Nadu is concerned it has established well coordinated structure at grassroots level immediately after tsunami struck. But it was purely a temporary structure. Even though the TNTRC, NGOs coordination cell, and District Resource Centres acted as coordinating structure among the NGOs and the Government, many of the NGOs were left out and they implemented their own agenda at Panchayat level. There was no coordination at village and Panchayat level. After tsunami struck, Government of Tamil Nadu issued a number of orders for relief, rehabilitation and reconstruction, but Government Orders didn't have legal binding. If Government or its officials were not implementing GOs people cannot bring them to court for redressal. The Government of Andhra Pradesh and the Government of Tamil Nadu and the Government of Gujarat didn't have separate department of Disaster Management.

Unlike Gujarat and Orissa, Tamil Nadu and Andhra Pradesh didn't have comprehensive disaster management policies. It didn't have policies for training elected representatives. The Government of Tamil Nadu trained a few elected representatives, community leaders and SHGs with the help of UNDP. Those were trained responded quickly and saved many lives when tsunami struck. The study found that the Government of Tamil Nadu lacks in the following areas, namely:

(a) Early warning system;
(b) Line of Communication and responsibility;
(c) Transparent and accountable governance;
(d) Preparation of contingency plans;
(e) Evacuation and rescue plans;
(f) Stock piling strategy;
(g) Transport of relief materials, damage assessment;
(h) Pre-positioning of food; and
(i) Targeting of vulnerable and specific groups.

Like Orissa, Gujarat also has separate structure called GSDMA but there is a lack of coordination between Government and NGOs. In Andhra Pradesh this lacking of coordination between NGOs and Government is evident.

3

Details of the Relief, Rehabilitation and Reconstruction Activities of the Government and Donor Agencies

This chapter explains the initiatives of the Government, Donor Agencies and Non-Governmental Organizations for providing relief, rehabilitation and reconstruction activities. After the occurrences of earthquake, cyclone, tsunami, floods in the four states, Donors and Government poured their assistance. It created significant changes in the social dynamics of the communities. Many felt that the assistance was poured more than needed. It was also felt and observed that benefits reached the real needy. This chapter makes an analysis of the kinds of relief reached, nature of relief provided, agencies involved in the relief, rehabilitation and reconstruction process, kinds of rehabilitation and reconstruction activities undertaken. Analysis has been made statewise and on a comparative basis also.

Orissa

Until 1999 with the few exceptions NGOs and other humanitarian organizations that were active in Orissa didn't specifically concentrate on Disaster Preparedness and management. Once the Super Cyclone hit the coast of Orissa in the year 1999, NGOs poured in cyclone hit areas. When devastating cyclones prompted the construction of cyclone shelters in the other coastal states of India, this was not in the case of Orissa. 1977 cyclone prompted Government of Tamil Nadu to construct cyclone shelters in all coastal panchayats. At the same time Government of Andhra Pradesh constructed more than 1000 cyclone shelters after the 1977 cyclone which killed some 10,000 people. In 1993, the German Red Cross conducted an assessment of cyclone preparedness among costal communities and the early warning system in Orissa. Because no major cyclone had struck Orissa for almost 20 years, the German Red Cross found it difficult to convince the donor agencies and the Government of India the urgent need for cyclone preparedness and construction of safe buildings. It was thus only in 1996 that the Orissa Disaster Mitigation Programme could be launched.

The Orissa Super Cyclone had hit Jagatsinghpur District on 29th and 30th October, 1999. The cyclone brought heavy rains which continued for over 36 hours. The maximum damage in this district was caused in Erasama Block of Kujam Tehsil. The block lying near the coast line was ravaged during the super cyclone. Experts have maintained an opinion that almost 90 per cent of the people who died in Erasama block during the Super Cyclone could had been saved if they have been evacuated as there was sufficient time with the state administration for evacuation.

The infrastructure facilities available in Orissa during and immediately after the Super Cyclone were grossly inadequate. In 1999, the whole district of Jagatsinghpur had only three cyclone shelters. The police wireless system in the region failed there were no radio masts which could withstand winds blowing at the speed of 260 to 300 km per hour. Also Orissa had no network of HAM radio sets at that time. These handicaps in terms of the infrastructure added with the lack of awareness on the part of local population in the affected districts proved too costly as about 10,000 lives were lost. The immediate response of the Orissa Government to the super cyclones in terms of rescue measures provision of relief and prevention of epidemics in the affected regions was dismal. The relief activities which followed have not been up to the satisfaction of all the victims even though the state received substantial assistance from humanitarian agencies other state governments and individual donors. The most victims, among the people seeking relief assistance had been the legal heirs of those people who received injuries during the cyclone and died because of such injuries later. Some such deaths had been compensated through *ex-gratia* assistance, but many cases were still pending and were being scrutinized by the district level committee. Also, no compensation was given to the people for the loss of livestock in the super cyclone though it was estimated the total number of livestock that perished in the super cyclone was about 4,40,000. The main reason cited was that official records of the livestock population were not there and hence it was impossible to verify the validity of any claim for such compensations.

In the 2001 flood, many of the godowns constructed by the government did not have relief materials by realizing this fate, government of Orissa started constructing godowns in 6000 gram Panchayats and also it ensured that adequate flood material was available. Apart from the godowns, government was constructing concrete roads.

After Super Cyclone in the year 1999, 50 competent organizations came together and thought about disaster preparedness and they established block level coordination. This mechanism was in place in the six districts. Those competent authorities established temporary structures with the following principles:

(a) Gender,
(b) Involvement of stakeholders,
(c) Dignity, and
(d) Transparency and accountability.

After the 1999 Super Cyclone the following relief materials have been distributed by INGOs and NGOs:

(a) Cooked food, rice, wheat flour, groceries,
(b) Tarpoulin sheets,
(c) Medicine kits, medicines, sanitation kits, bleaching powder,
(d) Blankets, sweaters, old clothes, old shoes, clothes, and
(e) Utensils, water filters, candles, bamboo cane and buckets.

Reconstruction Activities

NGOs which could mobilize resources continued with the longer team work in the field of construction of houses, schools and cyclone shelters. The construction of cyclone shelters became a major activity for NGOs active in disaster preparedness but community mobilization programme to ensure long term awareness among the beneficiaries and the proper use and maintenance of buildings were in many cases not included. In Ganjam block, Centre for Youth and Social Development (CYSD) constructed 21 school-cum-cyclone shelters with the support of the Netherlands (NOVIB) 17 with the support of SDC. It constructed two types of cyclone shelters. They are:

1. General, and
2. Stilt-double storied structure with the space—where livestock can be accommodated.

It facilitated to form construction management group and they are all selected from the community. They managed all construction activities. Display boards were put up. In that Display Board, the community updated the details like procurement and other details. Apart from the above village development community was formed. It worked under the construction management groups. Self Help Groups supervised the construction process. Once, the construction is over, it is handed over to shelter management and maintenance committee members. Around 7 to 11 members are there in committee. Rachana, part of the CYSD project, responded 2005, 2006, 2007 floods also. It distributed relief materials and organized community kitchens. It immediately responded and mobilized volunteers and deployed powers, boats to nine Gram Panchayats.

During the Restoration Phase

Many NGOs ensured food, food security for the people, repaired schools, repaired approach roads, renovated ponds, generated employment among people, planted trees on road side/avenues, and encouraged the communities to plant fruit-bearing trees at their backyards. Many NGOs facilitated the process of getting *kisan* credit cards for crop insurance. It also facilitated the formation of Pani Panchayat. Pani Panchayat groups checked the overflow of the water. It ensured equal distribution of water. Transfer of knowledge and techniques are important. In Kendrapada district, godowns were constructed in low lying area/low level plinths were put. These godowns were constructed as cyclone resistant buildings not as flood resistant buildings. For this drawback, one cannot blame Sarpanches.

All developmental projects should undergo disaster and environmental impact analysis. According to Gyan Das, Officer in OSDMA "when I was Block Development Officer, I never thought about disaster resistant buildings, disaster management and mitigation. I did not have knowledge". Government of Orissa has prepared vulnerability maps. Its ultimate purpose is to empower PRIs. It identified bottlenecks.

Institutionalizing Community Preparedness and Participation in Disaster Response

UNDP is implementing community-based disaster programme from the year 2001. In the community-based disaster management programme/plan, UNDP had many discussions with National and state governments. It was confined only in Orissa in the beginning. The Agricultural Ministry had dealt with community based disaster management programmes in the beginning. After the UNDP's constant effort it was shifted to the Home Ministry (Affairs). In the beginning, it was implemented in twelve states, and now it is being implemented in seventeen states. In these states, it is implemented in 169 districts.

At the Central level, the Home Ministry is the implementing agency. In a few states, they have a separate ministry or departments. In Tamil Nadu, the Revenue department is responsible for relief and rehabilitation. In Orissa, separate Department is there to transfer technology, knowledge and money. And also the Government of Orissa constituted Orissa State Disaster Mitigation Authority (OSDMA). OSDMA has direct contacts with district collectors. In turn, collectors contact Block Development Officers. BDO has contacts with village-level volunteers village volunteers work with stakeholders like PRI members, school teachers, CBO/NGOs. Special training programmes for PRI members are also conducted. Focus of the discussion in the training is on emergency centres, Control room and Civil VHF Network.

30 per cent of women participation is ensured in this programme. Government of Orissa with the help of the civil society organizations is celebrating October 20th as Orissa Disaster Preparedness Day. It was started in the year 2000. Every year special awards are given to the women DMT members.

The Non-Governmental Organizations as part of their reconstruction process have implemented community-based disaster management programmes. In that they prepared Community-based Disaster Preparedness Plans. After preparing the plan they discussed in Gram Sabha and Palli Sabha for approval. The trained disaster management teams (DMT) which came forward and volunteered in the rescue, relief and restoration activities, during the floods of 2001 and 2003 in the coastal districts of the state.

Disaster Resistant Agricultural Practices

They work on three areas, namely:

(a) Bio-farming,
(b) Disaster resistant seeds, and
(c) Adjusted varieties.

In the community-based disaster management programme, the study found that the following areas are to be strengthened:

(a) Women's participation/leadership in the disaster preparedness and response has been sustained. Of course, it needs to be strengthened;
(b) Revival of school as a part of relief/rehabilitation/mitigation process is important; and
(c) In the Orissa Disaster Management Policy, Panchayats do not have responsibility. But there is a provision that if there is hunger or chronic hunger, panchayats can provide rice for 10 days, i.e. food assistance.

As part of the reconstruction process, 50 competent organizations are involved in Disaster Preparedness Programme with the help of UNDP. The Block level coordination mechanisms were in 6 districts. Disaster preparedness was done based on the following five principles:

(a) Gender,
(b) Involvement of Stakeholders,
(c) Dignity,
(d) Transparency, and
(e) Accountability.

Mission Sakthi

In the Mission Sakthi Project, 3 days training was given to SHG members as masons and also 5 days training was given to engineers to construct disaster resistant structures. So far, sixty members have been trained, ten Master trainers have also been trained.

Red Cross

Red Cross is basically a voluntary organization. Volunteerism starts at school level as Junior Red Cross, at college level as Youth Red Cross and Red Cross Society. During disaster, Red Cross mobilized volunteers from schools, colleges, and from the villages. It closely works with District Administration, because Red Cross is headed by the district collector at the district level. As per the 2005 Disaster Management Act, the collector has to play a prominent role during disasters. During disasters, volunteers and trained persons were involved in searching operations and rescue work. In the 6 coastal districts of Orissa, 23 cyclone shelters were built by the Red Cross. It saved the life of 43,000 people during the Orissa Super Cyclone 1999. This cyclone shelters were built by the Indian Red Cross Society with the help of Spanish Red Cross Society and others. Experience from Bangladesh has shown that the construction of cyclone shelters doesn't automatically imply that they will be used by all community members, especially, women. Social mobilization and community awareness programmes were conducted in tandem with the construction of 23 shelters in all six costal districts. The German Red Cross supported the Orissa State branch of Indian Red Cross Society technically and financially for the social components of the programme, while the German Government through the German Bank for Reconstruction financed the construction of and equipment of shelters. Apart from building cyclone shelters, Red Cross responded to relief and rehabilitation activities, preparation of finance, initiated insurance among the affected people, initiated livelihood and other activities.

Apart from that, it conducted training programme, in the villages, prepared contingency plans. It trained shelter management committees, and a shelter management fund was established. The chairman of shelter management committee is the Sarpanch of the Gram Panchayat. A task force also established. The task force consists of volunteers, the sarpanch, Head Masters and ward members. The community contingency plan was prepared and up-dated time to time. Along with the regular activities mock drill were conducted (mock drill consists of how to face and manage disaster will also be performed). Each shelter had communication materials. There are two types of responses. They are:

(a) Quick response—Flood, cyclone and Earthquake; and

(b) Long-term response—Drought. One should have different approaches for both.

Box 4
Right-Beased Approach

CLAP is a NGO which concentrates on Human Rights violations in Disaster. After 1999 super cyclone CLAP sent a fact finding team to cyclone affected districts. It identified lots of human rights violations because of the non-responsiveness of the Government. They also found that the Government didn't properly pay relief amount to the next kin. Even though Government sanctioned relief amount there was delay in payment to the victims. In the Orissa relief code if officials violate the Government order or there was a delay in relief distribution, the officials cannot be punished based on the Orissa Relief Code. CLAP also found that there were violations of relief code. After the super cyclone, CLAP collected 1000 case studies within six months with regard to Human Rights violations in relief activities. It conducted public gatherings in front of the honourable judges. More than 10000 gathered on that day. One thousand victims of the 1999 super cyclone made disposition in front of the juries. They made it public that, rights of the people to get adequate compensation is important. Public hearing made the Chief Minister and the Chief Secretary to think in new ways. CLAP sent letters to various departments regarding the delays in payment of adequate compensation. 80 per cent of the victims were substantially provided necessary assistance If some departments were not providing adequate compensation, they were brought to the government's notice.

In Nimapura, a Block of Puri District, a Rural Welfare Institute (RWI) an organization introduced the Cash for Crop Project which was considered as a major source of livelihood and development of their village. In this project both men and women worked and got Rs. 70 equally. Through this project the community worked for their own village development such as laying of roads, reconstructing the damaged houses of the vulnerable without external fund, reconstructing the village ponds. This programme was introduced with the financial assistance from Concern World Wide, an INGO.

In Nimapura Block of Orissa Government sanctioned Rs. 75,000 for the family who lost their blood relatives but crop and livestock lost had not been considered. In the same Nimapura block of Orissa the Revenue Minister came and collected a list of the affected, according to that Government provided houses for those people. In some places, the Government through the Tehsildars has provided

Rs. 1000 for partially damaged houses and Rs. 2000 for fully damaged houses along with polythene sheets. In some places, the Government sanctioned amounts for the construction of buildings which were misused by the contractors.

Interaction with SHG members in Ichapur village, Olabode Panchayat, Balikuda block, Jagatsinghpur District

According to the Self-Help Group members, no relief materials from Panchayats and governments were available upto three days. People in this Panchayat took shelters in the College buildings. People got the information through radio. After the 1999 Super Cyclone, people collected coconuts and they shared them among themselves. Coconut was their first food. After taking coconuts, they reached safer places to settle down. After that food reached them. Neither the Panchayat nor government helped in the first three days. People searched for safer places, and had dry fruits to eat. There was no help from outside immediately after the 1999 Super Cyclone.

CYSD formed village development committees and facilitated one year with the help of Disaster Management Team (DMT), CYSD helped the community to prepare community contingency plans. Government entered only after 2 years. Before 1999 Super Cyclone, NGOs were very casual about disaster management. Now they have taken it very seriously. NGOs ensured the availability of food stock before each monsoon. Zilla Panchayat's prime responsibility was to give flood, cyclone tsunami warnings to all. It ensured putting food materials in all places. It ensured the people were evacuated and put in safer places. Zilla Panchayat also identified vulnerable points. They watched over the administration, whether district administration carry out its responsibilities properly or not. Zilla Panchayat put the pressure on district collector to carryout relief activities in time and quickly.

Table 3.1: Damage Caused by Super Cyclone of 1999 in Orissa, Extent of Damage

Total population affected	:	1 crore 29 lakhs
Total number of villages affected	:	14,643
Total number of Blocks affected	:	97
Crop area affected	:	18.42 lakh hectares
Total number of houses affected	:	19.49 lakhs

Table 3.2: Loss of Human Lives

District	*No. of Dead*
Jagatsinghpur	8,119
Cuttack	471
Jebdraoara	469
Puri	301
Jajpur	188
Bhadrak	98
Khurda	91
Dhencanal	55
Balasore	51
Keonjhar	31
Mayurbhanj	10
Nayagarh	3
Total	**9,887**

Total No. of People Injured	: 2507
Total No. of Persons Missing	: 40
Live stock Perished	: 4.44 lakhs
Fishing Boats Lost	: 9085
Fishing Nets Lost	: 2243

Table 3.3: Distribution of House Building Assistance

(A) Enumeration of Houses Damaged

Name of Tehsil	*Swept Away*	*Fully Collapsed*	*Partially Collapsed*	*Total*
Jagatsinghpur	0	62,647	19,542	82,189
Balikuda	902	60,611	7,371	68,884
Tirtol	85	31,808	10,267	42,160
Kujang	11,732	48,676	5,558	65,966
Total	**12,719**	**2,03,742**	**42,738**	**2,59,199**

(B) Total Disbursement of House-Building Grant

Name of Tehsil	*Swept Away*	*Fully Collapsed*	*Partially Collapsed*	*Total*	*Grant Total (Rs. in Cr.)*
Jagatsinghpur	0	62114	19290	81404	14.35
Balikuda	898	59784	7252	63934	12.99
Tirtol	85	30298	9678	40061	7.05
Kujang	11196	46405	5514	63115	13.75
Total	**12179**	**198601**	**41734**	**248514**	**48.15**

Table 3.4: Payment of Ex-Gratia Assistance

(A) Enumeration of Houses Damaged

Name of Tehsil	*Final Death Toll*	*No. of Cases Sanctioned*	*No. of Cases Rejected*	*Remarks*
Jagatsinghpur	154	144	10	The rejected cases are under re-enquiry
Balikuda	397	279	118	
Tirtol	149	129	20	
Kujang	6383	3580	2803	

Table 3.5: Distribution of Nets and Boats

(a) Inland Sector

Item	*Total No. of Beneficiaries*	*No. of Beneficiaries Who Received Money*	*Amount Disbursed*
Boats	992	645	Rs. 19.35 lakhs
Nets	1816	132\48	Rs. 20.22 lakhs

(b) Marine Sector

Item	*Total No. of Beneficiaries*	*No. of Beneficiaries Who Received Money*	*Amount Disbursed*
Boats	3022	2595	Rs. 77.85 lakhs
Nets	7052	4586	Rs. 68.79 lakhs

Tamil Nadu

As we have already discussed in Chapter 2, floods occurred regularly in Tamil Nadu, and a cyclone hit Tamil Nadu in 1977, which caused a major devastation. Whenever disasters occurred in Tamil Nadu, the Government of Tamil Nadu announced immediate relief packages. Once the Tsunami hit the coast of Tamil Nadu the Government of Tamil Nadu announced the following relief packages:

1. An ex-gratia payment of Rs. 1 lakh to the next kin of the dead person from the Chief Minister's Public Relief Fund. The above ex-gratia payment was given to the families of 6746 dead persons out of 7996 persons who died due to tsunami.
2. An ex-gratia amount of Rs. 1.55 crore was given to 169 missing persons from CMPRF out of 846 persons missing due to tsunami.
3. Rs. 3.5. crore as ex-gratia amount at the rate of Rs. 25,000 for persons who lost their limbs or eyes and at the rate of Rs. 5000

for those who sustained grievous injury. So far, 3504 persons have been assisted to the tune of Rs. 1.84 crore.

4. Relief package to 1,50,000 families who have lost their huts, at the rate of Rs. 4912 per family. The total amount allotted for this purpose was Rs. 73.68 crore. So far, 1,18,580 families have been benefited by this scheme at a cost of Rs. 58.25 crore. Relief assistance to the 15,000 families including the families of fishermen and those involved in small business and petty trades connected with the coastal economy at the rate of Rs. 2912 per family was initially sanctioned. This was further extended to 28,708 families at a cost of Rs. 8.36 crore. The amount has been actually disbursed to 1,78,708 affected families at a cost of Rs. 52.04 crore.
5. Rs. 5 crore was distributed as relief package for petty traders/ shop owners at the rate of Rs. 2000 for damages to mobile/ temporary shop owners and Rs. 5000 for damages to *pucca* shop owners. So far, 3762 small business owners have been assisted in Chennai and Cuddalore Districts.
6. Rs. 150.87 crore as sustenance allowance of Rs. 1000 and 30 kgs. of rice, provisions, kerosene etc., valued at Rs. 526 per month for each family for 4 months from February to May 2005 were given to the tsunami affected 3 lakh families. So far, 2,76,079 families at a cost of Rs. 37.70 crore for March 2005; 2,78,742 families at a cost of Rs. 37.81 crore for April 2005 and 2,79,429 families at a cost of Rs. 37.91 crore have received benefits. Total expenditure is Rs. 150.87 crore.
7. Rs. 52.76 crore worth of food grains allotted under the Rajiv Gandhi Rehabilitation Package of tsunami affected areas was adjusted with the sustenance packages of the Government of Tamil Nadu.
8. Rs. 47.71 lakh was sanctioned towards double ration of weaning food.
9. Rs. 9 crore was distributed towards a relief package of assistance to 1.5 lakh affected families who lost their houses by way of providing trunk boxes, stoves and stainless steel *kudams*. So far, 101023 trunk boxes, 98956 stoves and 101539 stainless steel *kudams* have been distributed at a cost of Rs. 7.04 crore have been given.

10. Rs. 10 lakh was sanctioned as relief to the Tamil Nadu Salt Corporation Ltd. for restoring the cross bunds inside the salt works in Ramanathapuram District.
11. Rs. 18 lakh as relief was sanctioned to nine damaged ice manufacturing units in Nagapattinam district.
12. Rs. 2,63,931 was sanctioned towards waiver of current electricity consumption charges of the ice manufacturing plants in Nagapattinam district affected by tsunami.

Table 3.6: Disbursement of Betel vine Assistance

Total number of Beneficiaries	:	6245
Number of Beneficiaries	:	4285
Amount Disbursed	:	Rs. 17.77 lakhs

The Government of Tamil Nadu sanctioned Rs. 1770 crores up to 28-2-2007 for relief and rehabilitation activities. These assistances were given sectorwise. In Fisheries Sector Government of Tamil Nadu sanctioned a sum of Rs. 65 crore from the Calamity Relief Fund. With regard to housing in the first phase 54653 partially and fully damaged houses would be replaced with disaster resistance houses costing Rs. 1.5 lakh each with built up space of 325 sq.ft. With regard to education free text books, note books and uniforms were disbursed to the students of 1st standard to 12th standard who were studying in Government/ Government-aided schools.

Kinds of Relief provided by NGOs and INGOs

Aluminum vessels, Bed sheets, Biscuits, Mats (New), New Steel Items, Rice Bag, Soap, Sugar, Tooth Brush, Tooth Paste, Water Packet, Wheat, Maida, Onion, Other Groceries, Syntax Tank, Dust bin, Bleaching Powder, Solar Lights, Dress materials.

Nature of Relief

Psycho-social Support, Education, Health and Nutrition, Shelter and Habitat, Water and Sanitation, Livelihood, Disaster Risk Management, Information, Communication, Technology and Coordination. Once tsunami news was heard by the NGO officials, they immediately contacted their field staff; to know the intensity of damage. Many NGOs provided dry food to all those affected. According to the staff of the World Vision, the District Collectors regularly conducted meetings. It provided food packet, rice, *Dal*, Sugar, Soap, Hygiene kit, Chair, Fan, Household materials and cooking materials. They took the affected persons-list from the village administration officer.

Apart from World Vision more than 700 NGOs came to Nagapattinam after tsunami struck. Before tsunami only eleven Governments approved NGOs worked in that district. After two and half years now 60 NGOs are working for reconstruction activities.

Box 5
Case Study of World Vision

World vision prepared a separate card for distributing relief materials. Whenever they distributed materials they got signature in the card and distributed. It distributed hygiene kit to 15 villages. World Vision concentrated on physically challenged persons. Most of its beneficiaries were physically challenged. World Vision constructed houses in 334 sq. ft. with 11 columns and 4 belts. They used 1.6 tonnes of steel rod. Land was provided by the community and infrastructure was provided by the government. Before they constructed the houses the list of beneficiaries was prepared in that beneficiaries list handicapped persons list was prepared separately. Whichever family had physically challenged people, they designed houses for the easy access of the physically challenged people.

Types of Work

1. Housing
2. Infrastructure facilities like construction of community hall and schools
3. Livelihood
4. Agricultural activities
5. Institutional based activities

In livelihood activities NGOs concentrated on fishermen, Agri labourers and dalits. Houses were constructed for fishermen only. Major housing activities were carried out by Amritananda Mayi Mutt, World Vision, Ramakrishna Mutt, TPG and TMSSS. NGO like CASA desalted the tanks. As far as HOPE Trust was concerned, they used various tools in the rehabilitation process. Their major tool was community involvement in the process of activities both in relief and rehabilitation. Discussion and interaction with the people gave sustainability to their activities. That has been taken for restoring normalcy. HOPE learnt several lessons in these relief works such as need-based activities and demand-based activities would minimize wastage and build confidence and restore self-dignity to the community. HOPE has been working in 15 villages around Pondicherry and Cuddalore. Their activities were on the psychological care of the children, child development activities, community organization for women, community organization for small and marginal farmers and welfare of the senior citizens. This organization made partnering with traditional panchayat leaders, tsunami relief committees, youth club and women SHGs.

A few NGOs who came to Nagapattinam for the relief and rehabilitation activities permanently settled there because they created assets like ITI, Community Polytechnic, Child Care Centre, etc.

As we have observed in the context of relief operations in the Tsunami hit regions of Tamil Nadu, certain preconceived notions of relief was forced up on the victims. For instance, relief efforts in Tamil Nadu witnessed endless provision of Sambar and Rasam rice, while people in the affected communities hardly wanted such food. This resulted from two factors. First of all, many of the agencies engaged in relief works were ill informed about the most affected people, the fishing community and its socio-cultural traditions, secondly, some of the relief efforts were not based on the felt needs of the victims rather they were supply-driven. With regard to rehabilitation activities many NGOs targeted the same families for different schemes.

Box 6

Status of Newly Constructed Houses in Trunami Affected Areas

The study found that once houses were ready in many places it took six months to get electricity. Another six months were taken to bring sewage facilities. But to many hamlets sewage facilities were yet to come. Everything just flows on to the streets or into the neighbour's backyard. All the houses have bathrooms, sealed up and closed because the septic tanks have been built (unusually, buried 3 feet underground level) without air ventilation pipes making them unusable. More alarmingly, not even in six month's old houses, huge cracks have appeared in many of the walls, near the foundation, on the roofs. Construction of Permanent house was delayed due to the unavailability of sites, disputes on the sites and caste conflicts.

The 2005 flooding occurred along the rivers and canals, it was the agriculture community who bore the brunt of the loss. Crops were destroyed and the river sand was deposited on the farm lands is severely threatening the people's food and livelihood security for the following year. Besides loss of crops many houses were damaged with the significant number of homes completely destroyed rendering 2,15,369 people homeless. Many of the families worst affected by the floods were from the poorest sections of the community. They had few assets besides their homes and survived predominantly on agriculture and agriculture related employment. The government responded by distributing rice and providing cash compensation. In total, this was a significant amount but spread across many people in Tamil Nadu. It amounted to very little per head. Most of the money was used to meet immediate needs rather than for rebuilding shattered livelihoods. The glaring difference between the size and scale of responses to this emergency as compared to the tsunami, left many questions about the way organizations, governments and individuals responded to disasters and what triggered a response. With very little loss of lives and without sudden and dramatic scenes as witnessed during tsunami there was little interest in the floods. The response from the organizations and government was negligible despite the fact that there were communities consisting of considerably poorer and more vulnerable than those directly affected by the tsunami. The massive funding, NGO presence and huge responses that were seen after the tsunami just did not happened.

Box 7
Case Study of Sanitation Facilities

In Kameshwaram Panchayat an ecological sanitation toilets-cum-bathroom complex with rainwater harvesting and solar panel lighting facility has been constructed. This was a joint venture of the Society for Community Organization and Peoples Education (SCOPE), FIN an NGO of France, Kameshwaram Panchayat, ETHOS, an architectural consultant of Kolkata and students of National Institute of Technology, Trichy. This is a model for joint venture between development organizations and panchayats.

Psycho-Social Care

SCARF has introduced tele-medicine services (tele-medicine is the delivery of medical treatment from the distance using information communication technologies). The study found that there is a dearth of trained mental health professionals and tele-medicine is the option for providing expert consultations. The study also found that the organization which is providing psycho-social care support does not have faith in traditional healing practices. Psycho-social care support is a western concept. The SCARF is distributing medicines once in 15 days in the entire costal area but patients are not aware of the medicines they are taking. Lack of clarity is seen among people on psycho-social support. Integrating disaster mitigation and management programmes with psycho-social support is important. Encouraging traditional healing practices is also equally important.

Box 8
Catholic Relief Services Intervention

"Tsunami took away my home, life was not easy in the temporary shelter. I had no toilets. I went to the bushes before dawn and waited for the sun to set. I was so scared of abuse. The community toilets constructed by CRS protected my dignity. I feel much safer now. The toilets are very clean now. I collect Rs. 5 every month as maintenance charge from the users to purchase disinfectants, equipments to keep the toilet clean. We use these toilets. They are important to us and hence we keep them clean".

—Jambrudh Nisha, Nagapattinam

Reconstruction

After Tsunami number of the Self Help Groups increased. Care India gave Rs. 3,400 worth materials. They distributed through SHGs. NGOs gave skill training in tailoring, candle making, driving, phenol making which were useful. SNEHA NGO gave Rs. 5000 for extending the house. But they were strictly told that those who have bank account only could avail of it. So everyone went to the bank to open a SB (saving bank) account. Even after waiting for one full day, they couldn't open the account. In many Panchayats, there were no special provisions for widows. After the intervention of SCORD all specially challenged persons got identity cards and got Rs. 10000 each. There are 32 specially challenged persons in Vanagiri Panchayat. Among them six were getting Rs. 400 per month.

Dalits

In Vanagiri Panchayat, Sevai NGO arranged food for dalits for the first one and half months. They all stayed at a *kalyana mandapam* for one week. They didn't receive any help from their Village Administrative Officer or from the Government. When they claimed their rights community problem arose. After a week, they made temporary shelters with their belongings like *sarees* and *dhoties* and accommodated lactating mothers and old-age persons. They took video of this situation and put it on websites. It worked very well. The NCC military arranged ten temporary shelters and NESA provided 72 temporary shelters. When they approached the panchayat president to arrange the land for permanent shelters, the place where they wanted to construct permanent shelters had been leased to the Spencer Company. So they took, the issue to the district collector. After seeing the Vanagiri map (jointly prepared by panchayat and HOPE NGO) the collector found that dalit's houses were not marked. Collector realized the scenario and he convinced the Spencer company to give the land to them. Now Oxfam has constructed permanent houses there.

Importance of ICT

PMSSS launched a five-minute special programme on All India Radio targeting fisherman and rural population. The programme was aired five minutes three times a day. They also joined hands with local TV channels like Skysat, Starplus and JVR to telecast information on weather and the waves. Lately, they deployed a Wave Rider Buoy system in collaboration with the Indian National Centre for Ocean Information Services, Hyderabad and National Institute of Oceanography, Goa. This system for the first time is being installed in the Union territory and provides information on tide height, wind speed, storm etc.

Early Warning System

With regard to the Information Communication Technology (ICT), there are three ICT centres, one in Panchayat and there is no coordination among themselves and they are not sharing the information. In Cuddalore district, the Early Warning Systems are not installed properly and in many places it was in the school buildings; if warning is given from the District Administration, there is no one at the receiving end. These EWS work only with electricity, during power failure the charge goes down, the system then collapses. The local representatives and committees are not trained properly in the use of EWS. The building keys of the EWS are with the constitutional Panchayat presidents/office, but they are far away from the villages, so the messages coming from the District Administration do not reach the villagers.

Table 3.7: The List of Village Loud-Speakers and Siren Installed

S. No	*Block/Village Panchayat*	*S. No.*	*Village Name*	*Location to be Fixed*
1.	Parangipettai Block	1.	Pitchavaram	Panchayat Office
		2.	Keezhaperambai and Keezhthirukazhipalai (Chinnakaraimedu, Veerankoilthittu)	Panchayat Office (Veerankoilthittu)
		3.	Pitchavaram Tourist Centre	Killai Town Panchayat Office
		4.	Kothattai	Self Help Group Office, Pudukuppam
		5.	Samiyarpettai	Cyclone Shelter, Samiyarpettai
		6.	Periyapattu	Multipurpose Shelter Kumarapettai
		7.	Mudasalodai	Government School
		8.	Muzhukuthurai	Government School
		9.	Melthirukazhipalai, Kavarapattu	Panchayat Officer, Kavarapattu
		10.	Jayakondampattinam	Panchayat Office Cyclone Shelter
		11.	Keezhakundalapadi	Cyclone Shelter, Ammankoil
		12.	Vallambadugai	Panchayat Office
		13.	Araganallur	Panchayat Office
		14.	Vadakumangudi	Old Water Tank
		15.	Nandimangalam	Panchayat Office

(*Contd.*)

(*Contd.*)

S. No	Block/Village Panchayat	S. No.	Village Name	Location to be Fixed
		16.	Elleri	Panchayat Office
		17.	Thirunaraiyur	Panchayat Office
		18.	Naanjalur	Panchayat Office
		19.	Edaiyar	Panchayat Office
		20.	Edaiyar	Panchayat Office
		21.	Thiruchopuram	Cyclone Shelter, Periyakuppam
		22.	Kayalpattu	Cyclone Shelter, Iyyampettai
		23.	Vandiampallam	Panchayat Office
		24.	Pudhampaadi	Panchayat Office
		25.	Sirupaalaiyur	Panchayat Office
		26.	Kothavacheri	Panchayat Office
		27.	Kundiyamallur	Panchayat Office
		28.	Adoor Agaram	Panchayat Office
		29.	Arangamangalam	Panchayat Office

Source: Computed.

Both the United Nations Development Programme (UNDP) and Center for Rural Education and Economic Development (CREED) have agreed for the objective of Capacity Building programme on Early Warning System (EWS) for six vulnerable blocks of Parangipettai, Kumaratchi Kattumanarkovil, Keerapalayam, Nallur and Managalore in Cuddalore District, Tamil Nadu. In these six blocks CREED has successfully covered all the Blocks for the EWS Capacity Building programme. This book envisages presenting the Programme objectives, Field Area profile, Participant Profile Course Assessment, feedback analysis and recommendations and photo profiles.

About the EWS Capacity Building Programme

Since the Government of India has declared that the Cuddalore is one among the multi-hazard prone districts of Tamil Nadu, the prime objective of this EWS Capacity Building programme is to save the lives and their property from the multi-hazards of the Target Area. UNDP and CREED have a partnership together to implement the EWS Capacity Building programme at six blocks of Cuddalore District. In this connection, UNDP conducted a two-day Master Trainer Training Programme for the partner NGOs at Anna Institute of Management at Chennai during July 2006.

In one village panchayat, namely P.R. Puram, NCRC, DHAN and MSSRF set up a Village Knowledge Centre, but there was no coordination between them and there was no exchange of materials among them. The research found that most of the time the Village Knowledge Centre was closed. They don't have contact with local NGOs and panchayats.

Box 9
Specially Challenged

In Vanagiri panchayat 8 specially challenged children are there. One Ms. Manjula stopped her education with 8th standard. If she wants to persue her study, she has to travel by bus which is difficult for her. After seeing her difficulty, SCORD NGO took her to Ayakudi, Thenkasi as exposure visit which has increased her confidence. She learnt livelihood activities and she is pursuing them.

NGO Coordination for the Right-based Approach

With regard to tsunami relief and rehabilitation measures, 93 civil society organizations from Tamil Nadu and Pondichery came together and gathered at Trichy on 31st December 2005 for an emergency meeting. The main purpose of the meeting was to ensure optimum use of human resources and money without duplication of intervention initiatives.

People's Watch, CEDA Trust and Tamil Nadu Women's Collective had taken the joint responsibility for organizing the meeting. The Trichy session ended in the creation of the tsunami relief and rehabilitation coordination (TRRC) as a policy influencing coordination to craft rehabilitation as a matter of right than of gratis of the state. The TRRC setup its head quarters at the People's Watch in Madurai, and within 6 months could increase its membership to 200 with about 300 members now. The TRRC has been recognized as the unit model deserving replication in any post-disaster relief and rehabilitation effort. The People's Watch is the only human rights organization to work for the excluded community in reaching relief to the batted survivors. TRRC was formally announced in Trichy on 10th December 2005. Hit and the affected were the term coined by the TRRC for taking up exclusion in relief as its first issue under collective scanner. The aim was to make the distinction between the victims who had suffered direct hit from the killer waves on the beaches and those whose livelihood was affected by the disaster.

Immediately after the tsunami, the Government and the NGOs were providing relief only on the costal communities mostly focusing on the fishermen forgetting the others affected by the tsunami. The TRRC undertook an elaborate and rapid impact assessment of this exclusion which later became the referral tool for many national and international bodies dealing with post-disaster help. At first, when the TRRC raised its voice against the neglect of the secondary impact of the communities. The government responded by saying there was no exclusion and stray cases if any could be brought before it for action by the end of January (2005). The TRRC completed its study of the excluded people and prepared a list of 6400 families affected by the tsunami but excluded in the relief operations. This list was given to the Government which announced its second phase of relief focusing only on these communities in February.

The public examinations of schools and colleges were due in March and April, but nobody was taking about the problems the victims faced. The waves have ruined their books and the relief camps had no space to sit and study. And also many schools in the costal areas were damaged. The TRRC organized the meeting of the affected people, NGOs and Government officials at Cuddalore in February and came out with two important demands: Postpone the exams for the 10th and 12th classes for the affected students so that they could get more time to prepare, waive all kinds of fees for the victim children for the next one year. A committee of educationist and other experts was formed. No TRRC member was included to draft the memorandum. It met the state education secretary, relief commissioner and other senior officials. The Government appreciated the initiatives and the very next day the necessary Government orders were issued postponing examinations for the tsunami children and waiving all the fees. Its first consultation meeting in Chennai on 26th January 2005 discussing the vital issues of public-private partnership to distributing the relief. Top government officials were present. The NGOs were disturbed by the government order stipulating that they should first deposit Rs. 75 lakh to bid for handling any housing project. That order meant that not only NGOs handling human suffering but any corporate could bid for the work and the spirit of public-private partnership to heal post-disaster plan could go haywire. It was the first door opening towards contracting and commercializing of the relief and rehabilitation tasks.

When the TRRC and its NGO members raised these objections, the government officials admitted that the order was a mistake and promised to withdraw it. However, it turned out that the government went ahead and signed the Memorandum of Understanding (MoUs) reiterating the original Government Orders, thus reducing the NGOs as social contractors in housing projects and thereby diluting their inherent philosophy of partnership with the beneficiary communities. It turned out that these building contractors had no clue as to who would be the beneficiaries living in those dwellings. The NGOs had already mobilized millions of rupees and that must be somehow spent. In the process, the works side of the NGO role in the post-Tsunami relief was demonstrated in the housing sector, where most organizations remained social contractors even to this day.

The TRRC also took up with the government the justified fears and stout protests from the fisher folks regarding the new stipulation that the new houses would be 200-500 metres away from the coast to ensure safety in any future disaster. "We thought this violated the fundamental norm that any rehabilitation should not be conditional," recalls a TRRC official. "Besides, there was apprehension among the NGOs, social activists and the fisher folks that once the communities were moved out of the beaches into their new houses farther away, they would be deemed to have relinquished their traditional rights over the coastline. Also, there was no guarantee that the beaches, thus cleansed of their traditional settlers, would not be allotted to the tourism industry for putting up hotels and recreation hubs."

"Right to the Coast", became the TRRC slogan, supported by a huge cross-section of coastal activities, including the Coastal Action Network, Sneha and Action Aid-India. The slogan accompanied the collective demand that the contentious GO-172 be scrapped. To cut short a long story of the TRRC struggle, alongside the other activities, beginning at ground level at the beaches and going right up to the chief minister's office and involving over 40,000 fishermen signing protest affidavits, the government finally gave in. The process of moving out the coastal families from the beaches stopped and no eviction was attempted after that.

A byproduct of that campaign was a study undertaken by the TRRC in all the Tsunami-hit districts to find out what the coastal community thought of GO-172. The study showed that the coastal people were clear in their minds that they would not allow themselves to be moved out of the beaches, whatever be the bait. Also, the TRRC campaigned for the allocation of proper land sites by the district administration so that the houses were completed and allotments made. The outfit took up instances, where the deserving got left out and 'outsiders' managed to sneak in—for instance, there was a case of a Chennai family being allotted a house in the Tsunami colony of Cuddalore.

The selection of the beneficiaries was done by the coastal panchayats (traditional leaders of the local community), so the TRRC took up consultations with these administrators during July-August 2005 and initiated corrective measures after some instances of misappropriation of funds and misjudgement of the beneficiaries happened. "We did not take recourse to any legal methods, like lodging police complaints and rushing to the courts, as that would break the social fabric and perhaps throw up fresh community conflicts," says the TRRC official. Next, the TRRC took up the task of ensuring quality of the boats gifted to the affected coastal families.

Also, TRRC was the first organization to review the Government of India Bill on Disaster Management when it was introduced in the Parliament in October 2005 (it was passed in December that year), in relation with the UN guidelines on resettling Internally Displaced Persons (IDPs) and adhering to the Sphere Standards, which are internationally recognized as being minimum standards and guidelines for relief and rehabilitation for disaster survivors, and, in line with the Gujarat State Disaster Management Act of 2003.

To sum up, the TRRC grew out of an urgent need for policy monitoring to ensure that procedures involved in relief and rehabilitation are fair, inclusive and appropriate for the communities affected. The coordination is founded on the principles of inclusiveness, active participation by all segments of society and the notion that strong communities provide the best foundation for creating sustainable livelihoods in the aftermath of a disaster.

Pursuing 'Policy-influencing' as the key agenda, the TRRC embraced a holistic, victim-centred approach that dealt with the psychological, economic, political and social aspects of the relief and rehabilitation effort. The TRRC worked at the state, zonal and district levels specifically to address the needs of vulnerable as well as the neglected groups. The organization focused its efforts on the able as well as the neglected groups. The organization focused its efforts locally, performing door-to-door needs' assessment to pinpoint exact needs, and tailored its response to individual communities. When those neglected lots failed to get heard and got left out of state aid and at times even overlooked by the NGOs, the TRRC helped identify them and brought them under care.

Box 10
Sanitation Agricultural Programme

The Hunger Project with the support of the Swiss Agency for Development and Cooperation, New Delhi, prepared a micro plan for rehabilitation in seventeen panchayats in Nagapattinam district. This initiatives is a participatory in nature and the process is based on the people centred approach throughout the project. This novel method of planning for social development. The first phase focuses on the first building through orientation, focus on panchayats as chief mediating agencies. The second phase concentrated on ensuring the continuing support of the Government departments, strengthening the panchayats through enhancing the pro-active participation by Dalits or women in the meetings, resolving conflicts between traditional and constitutional panchayats and partnership with other agencies.

The TRRC also made its mark in several sectors, including health, children, policy advocacy, media, housing, livelihoods, environmental impacts and trauma counselling and community support systems, besides caring for the Dalits, Adivasi (tribal) and minorities. The organization has also successfully completed ten research studies "with the objective of informing the underlying issues to a larger audience." Right from the

Impact Assessment Study following the Tsunami, the TRRC was able to manifest certain issues which were till then ignored—for instance, the extent of exclusion and discrimination of the marginalized communities from State relief—or unfocused (such as the enormous economic loss of the non-ocean fishing communities though spared of much physical losses). All these studies were "first of its kind in the State and were widely accepted within India and abroad," says a TRRC official.

True, the TRRC too had faced the "natural problems" of coordination where members needed to prioritize between their respective agendas and the common goal. "But at the end of the day, it was able to overcome all such problems and accomplish its mission," the TRRC official says.

The TRRC, needless to say, shaped a platform for the affected communities to assert and fight for their rights. By influencing policy, the organization sought to ensure that the victims got their rights. By influencing policy, the organization sought to ensure that the victims got their share of relief and rehabilitation without any discrimination. Interestingly, those drafting the TRRC document, stressed that such decisions not only ensured the success of the organization but were also practically possible. This TTRC case study is taken from the Turning the Tide-Touching the Lives of Neglected in Tsunami Recovery—United Nations, Care, Save the Children.

Positive Impact of Tsunami

(i) High quality of infrastructural facilities.
(ii) Development of Leadership qualities among children, youth.
(iii) Reduced drop out rates.
(iv) Increase of confidence level among youth.
(v) Level of interest increased among fishermen on education.
(vi) Improvement of health and sanitation facilities in the costal areas of Tamil Nadu.

Negative Impact on Tsunami

(i) Number of child marriages increased.
(ii) Relief materials poured more than needed.
(iii) Improper selection of livelihoods, e.g. in Akkaraipettai goats were given to fishermen. They kept all the goats in the temporary shelter. They don't know how to rear the goats.

Table 3.8: Details of Damages

S. No.	Districts	Population Affected	Houses/Huts Damaged	No. of Human Lives Lost	No. of Injured
1.	Chennai	73000	17805	206	55
2.	Cuddalore	99704	15200	617	198
3.	Kanchipuram	100000	7043	129	14
4.	Kanyakumari	187650	31175	828	727
5.	Nagapattinam	196184	39941	6065	1922
6.	Pudukkottai	66350	1	15	—
7.	Ramanathapuram	—	6	6	—
8.	Thanjavur	29278	3	33	482
9.	Thiruvallur	—	—	29	—
10.	Thiruvarur	—	—	28	—
11.	Thirunelveli	27948	630	4	4
12.	Tuticorin	110610	735	3	4
13.	Villupuram	78240	9500	47	30
	Total	**984564**	**126182**	**8010**	**3432**

Source: Department of Revenue, Government of Tamil Nadu.

(iv) Distribution of more boats than needed. This led to the shortage of manpower.
(v) Lack of need-based employment opportunities.
(vi) Tsunami cultivated negative mentality among fishermen, i.e. they always expected freebies.

Andhra Pradesh

The Government of Andhra Pradesh have taken long term measures with regard to tackling floods. It constructed 1000 cyclone shelters after 1977 cyclone that killed some 10000 people. If flood/cyclone struck, Government provides assistance like 20kg rice, 5 litres kerosene and Rs. 5,000. Panchayat has to inform mandal about the loss of property and life. According to the community, in Novapet village, Poodivaya Theru Panchayat, Vakadu Mandal, they get only 10 kg rice and 2 litres of kerosene. NGOs provided the following items:

(a) Fibre Boat,
(b) Motor Boat, and
(c) Net.

Many of the flood affected panchayats in Andhra Pradesh are near the reserved forest areas. They are opposing the laying of roads and other developmental activities. Self Help Groups are concentrating on many economic activities. NGOs are providing an amount of Rs. 15,000. SHGs are doing livelihood activities. In the village sustainable development committee, traditional Panchayats are dominating. In Thanakatta ST colony, their only communication network is through radio. There are 30 families living in this colony. They don't have *pucca* houses. After the tsunami, government decided to construct houses in this colony. The construction has started, but they are all at basement level. Socio-economic conditions are very poor in this ST colony. There is no Primary Health Centre, no school. They are struggling for their livelihood.

NGOs like Samatha, Speak India have been concentrating on disaster management programme from the year 1996. They work for flood management. But they also work for the rehabilitation of tsunami victims. They provided boats, nets and catamarans and helped the fishermen to get boats repaired. In the disaster management training they sensitized the importance of strengthening of bunds and the development of mangrove forest. Samatha NGO with the help of community has developed 50 acres of casurina.

Flood Management

In Khammam District—100 to 200 villages were affected by Godavari flood every year. If 53 feet water comes in Godavari all the river basins will be submerged in the months of August and September. In October 2007, the entire area was affected.

Table 3.9: Affected Mandals

S. No.	Mandals	Villages
1.	Rargambadu	1
2.	Kukunoor	4
3.	Vellerupedu	5
4.	Konavaram	4
5.	Chintoor	4
6.	Dummugudam	4

Source: Compute.

First their fields were submerged. Later, their houses were submerged. In 2006 floods, all the 21 villages were submerged in the floods. Fields were filled with sand. People packed all their important personal valuables and were shifted to upland area. They went and stayed in temporary shelters. Schools were converted into temporary shelters. Sometimes, when the entire villages were marooned, food packets were thrown from helicopters.

In the temporary shelters and flood affected areas, government provided 5 litres of kerosene, 10 kg rice, tamarind, chilli powder, cloth and turmeric. This was a temporary relief. They stayed there up to 10 days. After flood receded, people went back to their own houses. Government provided nominal amount for crop damage. Rs. 700 per acre was given to purchase seeds. NGOs conducted health camps. Officials went by boats for relief activities. The communication system was affected during Godavari floods. Livestock were also washed away.

Local elected representatives, CBOs, NGOs and ward members VRO, MPTCs, Sarpanch went and rendered their services. With regards to relief measures, all the people were not covered. Identifying the affected people was a big task. The committee helped those people affected by the flood. 7 to 11 persons were the members of the committees. Four women were there as member, representatives from gram Panchayat and other CBOs were also there.

These Committees regularly met and identified the damages. Whatever help they got, they disburse them through this committee only. Many NGOs carried out their activities through these committees. They are:

(a) Forming committees—village level flood management committee,
(b) Survey committee,
(c) Identification of affected families by a committee, and
(d) Gram Sabha meeting.

Social audit was conducted in many villages, the survey included:

(a) house damage,
(b) crop damage,
(c) cattle damage, ..
(d) domestic materials damage,
(e) working days damage,
(f) land damage, and
(g) health damage.

NGOs Intervention

Most of the NGOs formed committees. Whatever the budget they got from the outside, and they showed to the committees. The Committee members decided the materials to be purchased and they purchased and distributed them among themselves. In a few villages, they (where NGO intervention was there) collected Rs. 100 from each family and put it as relief fund. The panchayats deposited the amount in the bank. They utilized this amount during the flood. A few NGOs gave training to the farmers on sustainable agricultural methods, motivated farmers practiced Non-Pest Agriculture (NPA) methods which reduced the cost of cultivation.

Relief by NGOs

The NGOs distributed the following:

25 kg rice, blankets, *sarees*, blouses, *dhotis*, towels, cooking oil/*dal*/ dettol bottles. A compensation of Rs. 1500 for the fully damaged crops, Rs. 1000 for the partly damaged crops were given. Agricultural products

like chilly, green gram, red gram, black gram, maize, submersed in water. Seeds were given at 50 per cent of subsidized rates. NGOs were concentrating on the following activities:

- (a) linking the government programmes with the affected families;
- (b) helping petty businesses;
- (c) providing crop loans;
- (d) running general stores;
- (e) farming (many women were interested in farming); and
- (f) poultry and dairying for the landless agricultural labourers. Village level committees were empowered to do policy making to implement the government flood management programmes. Because of the floods, a few families were suffering from health problems continuously. Gram Sabha was conducted in few villages to decide the next course of action.

To generate awareness about health, posters were displayed. They were about:

(a) pregnant women,
(b) healthy food,
(c) nutrition cycle,
(d) training ANM, and
(e) nutrition for children.

Gram Panchayat level government structures have the following components:

(a) Sub-centre;
(b) Anganwadi centre;
(c) Mandal Level: Public Health Centre;
(d) Block Level: Area Hospital; and
(e) District Level: Speciality Hospitals. Communities are motivated to utilize the services.

Burugambadu Mandal, Pettaraikundam Panchayat, Venkatapuram SC Colony

Flood committees were formed by SECURE NGO. Nine members were there, 4 males and 5 females. In the Venkatapuram SC colony, lands around the village were only Patta lands and all the other lands belonged to the reserve forest. Scheduled Caste people depend on the reserve forest for their livelihood. During the Godavari flood season, there was no work and so there was a shortage of food. One person died without treatment in the last year's Godavari flood season. The village secretary and the village servants got the relief packages from the government. Only some people managed to get these packages. Others were left out. There was no cooperation among the people to get relief packages.

Box 11
Sustainable Agricultural Programme

Non-pesticide management methods. Two village farmers stopped using pesticide. A farmer from Gundur took lease of lands and did cotton cultivation by using lot of pesticides. But the crops failed. 60 farmers committed suicide. By using neem seed oil, neem seed powder, ginger cow dung, sustainable agriculture was practiced. The Agriculture minister sanctioned ginning mills. Farmers directly sold their products.

Gowdiniya Mukthi/Seevazhi/Kukunoor, Khammam District

All the hamlets in these Panchayats were affected by the flood. All families in this SC colony, packed their valuable items and settled temporarily in the nearest safer places. They came back after one week. Government allotted 20kg rice per family during flood time as a relief package. Only a few families got 20kg of rice. Others got only 4 or 5 kgs. Every year, because of these floods in the Godavari there were crop failures. After that, they grow only pulses. Once flood receded, their land becomes very fertile whatever they grow would give them good returns. With regard to temporary shelters, community constructs their own tents. Last year for 10 to 15 days, the water level did not recede, hence they cooked their food. They were satisfied once the government assessed the damages. They were not much worried, whether they were getting compensation or not. In Khammam District in the Godavari belt, many of the SC colonies were near the reserve forest area. So they could not shift their hamlets to nearby area because their livelihood depended on the forest lands.

During flood seasons, women were the worst victims. There won't be electricity. Lack of toilet facilities which made them much vulnerable. Shortage of food was also there. Shortage of fire woods was also a problem. They used Rice and Jowar alternatively. Lots of snakes came during floods. People bitten by the snakes were taken to the nearby hospital (3 kms from the Panchayat). A RMP practitioner was there to treat them. *Pucca* hospital is 15 km away from the place. Local revenue officials distributed relief materials only to a few villagers.

Formation of Self Help Groups and providing loans for their livelihood activities were the main rehabilitation works done by all NGOs. A few NGOs provided Rs. 3,000 for house construction. Village level flood management committees were formed by the NGOs, but they did not have any connection with the Gram panchayats. The village level flood management committee identified the beneficiaries and prepared the budget. The government of Andhra Pradesh has spent Rs. 4,000 crores for Godavari delta modernization. For strengthening of the bunds it spending Rs. 620 crores from Thavaleswaram to Erithralanka.

Most of the NGOs formed groups at village level, such as task force, warning team, protective team, first aid team, rehabilitation team and distribution team. The Samatha NGO formed a network called elected women's network. Through this it develops the capacity of the EWRs, analyses the gender problem, and creates awareness regarding women's rights.

Suggestions from NGO Representatives

In the Nellore district of Andhra Pradesh, the traditional structures and systems are very strong, traditional leaders and village strongholds did so much atrocities on women. Most of the villages in Nellore district did not have trained doctors and health workers in the year 1986. It is a highly feudalistic society. Speak India had plans to protest against these atrocities in a Gandhian way from the year 1986. With the affected women, Speak India went on a hunger strike for 27 days against the atrocities on women. For the appointment of the lady doctors, it went on a hunger strike for 17 days. Women are very vulnerable in Nellore district. After the Speak India's constant struggle, police started filing cases against culprits for rape etc. The state government has recognized the Speak India organization.

In 1993, after Latur earthquake tragedy, Speak India worked for flood relief in 1996 in Prakasam District and in 2001 floods in Nellore district. In case of any disaster in Nellore District, Speak India responded immediately. November is the black month for Nellore District. Upland areas were more vulnerable in the 2001 flood, big bridges were washed out in the Rapur, which is a hilly area.

Backwater

Now-a-days, government, NGOs and international agencies are not concentrating on maintaining water bodies and catchment areas. If the channels are restored sufferings of the people will be mitigated. Now-a-days, water bodies are not in a position to recharge; they are only discharging. Government should plan for the vulnerable areas. People and animals should be safe. In the cyclone shelters there are no separate toilet facilities for women, no maintenance fund, no one is there to redress their grievances, no committee is formed. Without enough resources, people cannot develop their skills.

The Speak India organization helps villagers to have sustainable development. Trained community leaders should be provided with life jackets. Special needs of the women should be addressed. Women feel it difficult to escape, because of their dress pattern. Women's special needs should be addressed during disasters.

Disaster occurs every year in the same fashion. If we concentrate on small things like: desilting of tanks and for this two methods can be followed:

(a) Regular approach and (b) Geographic approach. The feelings of the people should be respected. Desilting and deepening of tanks, rebuilding the sleuths and bunds should be undertaken for speedy discharge of water.

Gujarat

Considering the enormous direct and indirect losses caused by the earthquake, the reconstruction and the rehabilitation programmes will require a total outlay of about Rs. 8,500 crore (US $ 1770 million). The government of Gujarat proposes to secure a loan of about Rs. 3,300 crores (US $ 687.5 million) from the World Bank and Rs. 1680 crore (US $ 350 million) from the Asian Development Bank. Government of India and the number of state governments have declared their support and contribution for various components of the rehabilitation programme. The government of Gujarat proposes to meet any shortfall in the reconstruction programme through its own resources.

Box 12
Health System

While interacting with the communities, it was observed that, in many villages there was no primary health centres (PHC). They have to travel a long way for the PHC, where they have no proper roads.

After the earthquake struck Kutch and Bhuj, the State Administration gave food kit, comprising 50 kg of flour, 3 kg of Potatoes, 2 kg of Onions and Salt to each family in Gandhi Nagar and Bhuj. Potable water pipes were repaired within four days. The government of Gujarat sent the Additional Chief Secretary to Bhuj by helicopter to supervise the relief measures.

Health: A System that Never Stopped

The first and foremost task in the affected areas was to restore the health system back to its routine function so as to bring back hope. The hope was brought back by making all health units functional immediately in 4,134 temporary and alternative arrangements. More than 17,000 injured were treated immediately. All hospitals and health units were made functional immediately. Orthopaedic rehabilitation of more than 8,000 handicapped persons was undertaken by supplying crutches, walkers, seats, calipers, artificial limbs and tricycles. Financial assistance was given to the injured and the handicapped depending on the degree of injury and handicaps. Special monthly pension of Rs. 2000 for all the 105 para plegic cases and continuous therapy and treatment. Repairs of 2,225 anganwadis and reconstruction of over 430 health buildings were also taken up.

Assistance for Revival of Agriculture

Assistance up to 60 per cent towards the repair/reconstruction cost for all the affected tiny, small, medium and large scale industries in seismic zone IV and V, and 50 per cent assistance for other zones were distributed. Interest liabilities have been given for existing loans from financial institutions. For those affected traders, businessmen and professionals who invested above Rs. 2 lakh was provided with a maximum subsidy of Rs. 1.2 lakh in seismic zone IV and V whereas it was up to Rs. 1 lakh for the other zones.

Over fifty-eight thousand farmers were provided with input kits containing tarpaulins, spray pumps, farming tools, storage rooms, seeds, chemical fertilizers and pesticides, and farm structures like engine rooms and the store rooms for 47,000 farmers. Irrigation facilities like tube wells, motors were given to more than 75,000 farmers. 16030 women were targeted as beneficiaries under women livelihood restoration project. 2500 women were provided with aid for self-employment. Despite these, there was Micro Insurance (crop insurance), it did not meet even the loan amount borrowed by the farmers.

Infrastructure

Under the Gujarat earthquake, reconstruction and rehabilitation programme the government of Gujarat implemented a massive programme of infrastructure rehabilitation and improvement. The objective of the programme was to improve infrastructures beyond the pre-earthquake level and to reduce the susceptibility to future disasters. It involved application of disaster resistant technology in repairs, strengthening and reconstruction.

Inclusion

Orphans and Children of Single Parents

Compensation was paid to 1758 orphaned children on the death of either or both parents in the form of joint account of Collector/DDO and the child. 91 children were provided with monthly assistance of Rs. 500 under the foster parent scheme. A surveillance mechanism was established with the help of UNICEF and NGOs to keep a regular track of well-being of the orphans. A total of 14 child lines were established with the help of National Children's Fund. Five of these are in Bhuj, Anjar, Rapar, Bharuch and Gandhidham, which are run by the local NGOs for providing assistance to destitute women, children as well any person who is in need of help.

Widows and Old Persons

999 widows and 651 old persons were covered under the monthly pension scheme. Three old age homes are functional in Bhuj, Bhachau and Anjar.

Disabled

Disability cards have been issued to 830 disabled persons, which entitled them to avail themselves of the various concessions and facilities. 3017 supportive devices were provided to the disabled people through Blind Peoples' Association funded by the Ministry of Social Justice and Equality, Government of India.

Box 13
AIDMI Intervention Made a Peaceful Life for Rasheeda

Rasheeda is 28 years old, six persons are living in her house (she, her husband, mother-in-law and three children, among three children, one is adopted children). The children are very young, two children are studying. Before intervention of AIDMI, she and her husband were casual labourers. Their income was not sufficient even to meet the daily expenses. So they were compelled to seek the help of the money lenders. Money lenders extended financial assistance with high interest rates and also they shouted at them if they failed to pay the daily installments. So they had worries in mind. They were unable to have a peaceful life and also unable to sleep weli in the night. After AIDMI's intervention Rasheeda was trained in making readymade materials. So now they are able to save Rs. 500 per month, apart from that saving they are able to pay Rs. 290 as insurance every year. Also they are paying the loan installment amount of Rs. 1,200 without default. She proudly says, "Now we got some social status".

Women's Participation in Construction Work

One of the house in Bhuj village was destroyed (about 80%). Everyday both the husband and wife started constructing the house and completed the house within 5 days. They think that if they waited for any external agency, it might have taken a long time. Meanwhile, the women were given training for mason work. Thus, if women are involved in the reconstruction work, they work very well and they need not depend on government or on NGOs. Thus masons and engineers were trained for multi-hazard resistant housing reconstructions. Over 29,679 masons and 6,500 engineers were trained.

Box 14
Housing

The government's housing recovery policy calls for a participator, community-driven process, with community and individual households rebuilding on a self-help basis, with technical support and facilitation from government, private sector, NGOs, local government and the Panchayat system. The government and the NGOs had assessed the damage with the people's participation and categorized into five—G1, G2, G3, G4, G5. The Gujarat State Disaster Management Institute approved Rs. 8,000, Rs. 15,000, Rs. 30,000, Rs. 45,000 and Rs. 1,50,000 to G1, G2, G3, G4, G5 respectively. The Gujarat Disaster Management Authority had 30 types of model houses, from which the beneficiaries had freedom to choose anyone.

Rehabilitation

The biggest ever housing reconstruction programme was undertaken in the entire world in terms of numbers and geographical area. Housing assistance packages were announced in a record time. Repairs of all the 9,08,710 houses were completed and 1,97,091 houses were reconstructed out of the destroyed 2,22,035 houses. By public-private partnership programme 36,901 houses were constructed. One NGO was involved in constructing shelter activities. It collected Rs. 4000 from each beneficiary and created an account for Disaster Management. But the drawback was the communities do not know how much was collected and deposited.

Box 15
Status of Temporary Shelters

The communities felt only one drawback in housing rehabilitation process. It was that they got power supply after six years. While staying in temporary shelters, the food prepared by us was destroyed by dogs and cows because the temporary shelter was not that much safe, so we struggled a lot during that time. The government provided temporary shelters only after four to six months in some areas. The government gave option that either they can stay in the temporary shelter or they can stay somewhere else, for that they provided Rs. 1500 for rent. In some rehabilitation areas, the current supply was given after six years.

Education

The Government of Gujarat has not restricted its efforts on reconstruction and rehabilitation of houses and health service, it also extended its services to the other activities such as education. Through these activities, 50,890 damaged class rooms were reconstructed and nearly 4,000 class rooms have come up anew. All the new class rooms are multi-hazard resistance with amenities like safe drinking water, child-friendly spaces and furniture and space for sports activities. The recovery programme not only covers primary education but also higher, technical and medical education.

Rural Water Supply

Against this background, twenty water supply schemes were launched. 222 tube wells were drilled in 152 villages. 2126 km pipelines were already laid for the water supply schemes. 543 related civil structures have been completed. Rural water supply schemes were planned and implemented at village level with the participation of NGO/CBOs. Use of hazard resistant construction technology and materials with specifications for earthquake resistance was insisted, replaced damaged pipes with corrosion resistant metallic pipes with flexible joints. Demand projection has been made for 30 years while planning of the system.

Power

Power was restored partially to the Bhuj town by 28th January and to the other 8 towns by 30th January 2001. Power was restored in stages in the affected 925 villages by 2nd February 2001. Over 2557 kms of transmission network and 2676 kms of distribution network were repaired and strengthened. Repairs of all the 465 transmission equipments in the districts of Kutch, Rajkot, Surendranagar, Jamnagar and Banaskantha have been completed. Reconstruction of 64 buildings has been completed and the rest 133 buildings are in progress.

Early Warning System

There is no Early Warning System in the villages. Through radio and Television only they communicate about the disasters but the news reached them only after the flood rushed into the villages, even though it helped them to know about the intensity of the flood. But, sometimes, due to power failure they were unable to know the news. The Block Development officers communicated, but not to all villages. The roads were blocked for seven days. They were unable to communicate with government officials because of power failure they were not able to recharge the mobiles.

Reconstruction

Livelihoods

The earthquake rendered many not only homeless but also jobless. Restoration of livelihoods is one of the most important aspects of Gujarat earthquake reconstruction and rehabilitation programme, which made the programme truly all encompassing. Government did not merely aim at restoration of livelihoods but all the efforts were being made towards providing sustainable livelihoods and reduction of economic vulnerability by empowering women. The livelihood programme was offered in two types, one is short term recovery assistance and another one is long term economic assistance. In short term recovery assistance up to Rs. 2 lakhs

Box 16
AIDMI Interventions

AIDMI, in Gujarat, wants to promote the livelihoods to the affected people to have sustainable lives. So it gave livelihood supports to the people. Their need were based such as saloon shops, petty shops, cycle shop, etc. The AIDMI, also promotes Micro Insurance such as weather insurance and Disaster Insurance, food for cattle.

was provided as loan to self-employed people for village and cottage industries through commercial banks and financial institutions with 60 per cent subsidy, Rs. 2,500 for purchasing of tool kits, up to Rs. 5,000 for construction of temporary work sheds. Special attention was given to weavers and handicrafts men.

In the long term economic assistance for artisans who had lost their work shed, government provided them with permanent work sheds of 20 to 25 sq. m with no contributions from the beneficiaries. Formation of rural industries development centres at 50 locations for providing infrastructural assistance at a cost of Rs. 4.5 crores and with a partial assistance for a formation of 24 mini handloom handicraft parks in affected area at a cost of Rs. 1 crore were undertaken. Likewise 8 district level handloom handicraft parks at a unit cost of Rs. 2 crore were started.

Dam and Irrigation

Three major drinking water supply dams, 19 medium and 160 minor irrigation schemes in Kutch and 67 dams in Saurashtra were started. Their constructions were completed before the onset of the monsoon of 2001. The Aga Khan Foundation involved the communities for two different reasons; one was to generate employment opportunities and the second one, was to make them work hard, in order to make them tired which will made them to forget all the worries and made them to sleep well. This was also another type of psychological treatment. Public buildings constructed: 8,890 public buildings have been repaired and 2,456 buildings were reconstructed. In all the buildings the multi-hazard resistance features and rain water harvesting systems were fixed. Over 3,600 km of state highways and rural roads were strengthened.

Public Health and Public Buildings

Even though, over all 5,000 buildings belonging to the public health system were either damaged or destroyed, the health system never stopped functioning.

Public Buildings

8890 buildings were repaired and 2456 buildings were reconstructed. All the public buildings being reconstructed had multi-hazard resistant features. Implementation of rain harvesting system in all the projects of police housing was carried out. Other than repairs and reconstruction, retrofitting was also taken up for ensuring safety in future disasters and also they had a demonstrative effect to build confidence in the affected people.

Third party quality assurance and Technical Audit for Repairs, Reconstruction and Retrofitting to ensure quality were arranged. The valuable exhibits including the gold crown inlaid with precious and semiprecious stones were salvaged successfully from the Bhuj Museum by the Archaeological Department. Financial assistance ranging from Rs. 50,000 to Rs. 500 lakhs was distributed to owners of private heritage buildings for restoration.

Traditional Knowledge of Building Houses

The community people in the Thuga village of Kutch district were given land by the government, after their houses were damaged in the earthquake and where they asked for relocation. People moved to the relocated area, and waited for one month. But no one came for construction works. After a long while, the community took initiative in constructing houses themselves with the left out materials from the old place. By seeing the community's coordination, Kutch Mahila Vikas Sangathan and NGO helped them in the construction work. Thus people had the traditional knowledge of how to build houses called 'Bhunka' which is like a round shaped wall, plastered with small road supported by bamboo sticks. Though the construction was completed they were not provided with electricity facility for which they had to wait for another six years. After a long time, now they are enjoying this facility.

Self-Help Group Formed, No Disaster Preparedness Training

In Gujarat, every village had Self Help Group formed by the organizations like SEWA and Kutch Mahila Vikas Sangathan (KMVS). They were carrying out various developmental activities through community participation. After the earthquake, SHGs were formed as a mobilizing tool for earthquake rehabilitation. But they were not trained for any disaster preparedness.

Preparedness as a way of life

Government of Gujarat initiatives are explained hereunder. They are:

(a) Gujarat State Disaster Management Act was enacted on 13 May 2003;

(b) "Emergency communication plan" and "community strategy and media plan have been prepared";

(c) Emergency response centres were to be established in Ahmedabad, Surat, Rajkot, Vadodara and Bhuj;

(d) A network of 22 seismological observatories and 40 strong Motion Accelerographs were to be established/upgraded at different locations across the state;

(e) Resource Network of more than 18,000 villages has been created in SDRN (State Disaster Management Network);

(f) GIDM has already conducted over 39 training programmes covering over 1292 trainees;

(g) A chapter on Disaster Management has been introduced in the First year of the P.T.C. syllabus by Gujarat Centre for Educational Research and Training (GCERT) from the educational year 2004-2005;

(h) Maintaining up-to-date information about population, livestock, housing, crops and other assets. It should be maintained in village Panchayat as well as with district office. Likewise, village disaster management plan should be prepared;

(i) Sounding the early warning to make all village people residing in vulnerable areas to shift to safer place and also helping them in identifying and establishing relief camps;

(j) Special attention should be given to expectant mothers, physically challenged and old age people;

(k) Storage facilities for food, medicine, water, clothes, agriculture raw products in every habitations should be provided;

(l) Panchayati Raj Institutions need to be trained to evolve a community-based disaster preparedness and plan;

(m) Panchayat Raj Institutions should be given awareness in gender and vulnerability focus;

(n) The roles and responsibilities of Panchayati Raj Institutions should be explained clearly; and

(o) Panchayat Raj Institutions should be trained in using the locally available resources and organizations during the time of disaster.

Retrofitting Technique

The houses were partially damaged and they needed retrofitting technique. People were not aware of this technique and started repairing with local method which did not ensure seismic safety and in some cases, people pulled down their houses in order to have earthquake resistant houses. Abhiyan initiated a retrofitting project with the support of Centre for People's Action for Disaster Preparedness (CPDP). A Latur-based organization which played a significant role in spreading awareness about the importance of retrofitting and disseminated technical information. In Collaboration with Abhiyan, the organization conducted a massive campaign with the Setu through video shows and poster exhibitions. It also gave mason training (The Setu is a network of nodal points for facilitation of relief and rehabilitation process in Kutch for a defined geographic cluster of 15-20 villages each). These Setus have been supporting CPDP and Abhiyan in identifying the houses requiring retrofitting treatment.

Table 3.10: Loss of Human Lives Caused by the Bhuj Quake of 2001 (as on 26-2-2001)

S. No.	*District*	*Human Deaths*
1.	Ahmedabad	751
2.	Amreli	00
3.	Anand	00
4.	Banaskantha	32
5.	Bharuch	09
6.	Bhavnagar	04
7.	Gandhi nagar	08
8.	Jamnagar	119
9.	Janagarh	08
10.	Katch (Bhuj)	18414
11.	Kheda	00
12.	Mehsana	00
13.	Navsari	17
14.	Patan	38
15.	Porbandar	09
16.	Rajkot	433
17.	Surat	46
18.	Surendranagar	113
19.	Vadodara	01
20.	Sabarkantha	00
21.	Valsad	00
Total		**20,003**

Table 3.11: Relief Measure taken following the Bhuj Quake

(Immediate Relief) Cash dole	Rs. 2,000 per person
Compensation for Death	Rs. 1 Lakh
Compensation for Injury	Rs. 50,000
Housing Aid	Rs. 90,000
Work shed Aid for Craftsmen	Rs. 10,000

Table 3.12: Relief after the Earthquake of 2001

Compensation for Death	20,000 persons (approx.)
Injury assistance	19,648 persons
Cash assistance	9,11,096 families
Household kits	3,72,000 families
Provision of temporary shelters	3,48,626 families
Total rubble removed	17 lakh truck loads

Source: Socio-economic Review, Gujarat State, 2001-02.

To sum up, disaster like floods are regular phenomenon, but NGOs and INGOs are not much sensitized on this as far as Tamil Nadu is concerned. In Andhra Pradesh NGOs and Government are not giving importance to Panchayats, even though panchayat leaders are part of the flood management committee. When district collector convened the flood management committee meeting, many leaders were not present. Many Gram Panchayat leaders in Orissa, Gujarat and Andhra Pradesh were not aware of the development schemes. Reconstruction activities like establishment of infrastructure facilities like laying of roads, construction of schools, health centres, laying of pipes and electrification are very poor in Orissa. But they are involving community-based disaster management programmes. One reason for the lack of preventive action in Orissa might be that the Orissa Relief Code of the State Government paid little attention to the role of NGOs in disaster preparedness and response before 1999 Super Cyclone. In any disaster, INGOs and NGOs have plans for only three years. They have an urge to spend the allotted amount. In Tamil Nadu, NGOs and INGOs never thought beyond the distribution of boats, nets and construction of houses. While distributing relief materials, they lack gender sensitivity. No one distributed baby food, essential medicines, special clothes for women. One NGO Medicine Sanfrantis, winded up its activity within three days from the tsunami affected areas. It realized that it didn't have space to work.

According the Ms. Bimla Chandra Sekar, EKTA, there is a missing dimension of Gender in relief and rehabilitation activities carried out through both Government and NGO initiatives. She further highlighted that more women have been affected in disasters compared to men both in terms of numbers and intensity. She shared from her experiences she gained while interacting with the affected women in tsunami affected areas that nobody asked about the physical problems of women affected in tsunami. She indicated the reasons for women being affected more than men. She explained that using instances from the other states that, while carrying out activities during natural disasters we have to carry out activities keeping gender in the backdrop. While analyzing the relief, rehabilitation and reconstruction measures in the above four states this study found that INGOs, NGOs and the Government didn't consider women, children, physically challenged and people suffering from illnesses. NGOs and INGOs have not distributed live saving medicines, milk powder, baby food, materials needed for women and dresses suitable for women.

4

Involvement of Stakeholders in Relief, Rehabilitation and Reconstruction Activities

In the previous two chapters, the perspectives of the organizations, institutions and government, relief and rehabilitation activities, details of relief, rehabilitation and reconstruction activities of the government and donor agencies were analysed and discussed. In this chapter we examine whether the stakeholders involved in relief, rehabilitation and reconstruction activities, reasons for involving and not involving, whether there is coordination from the panchayats to state level. Once the reasons for the above said issues are analysed suggestions could be drawn from the analysis to involve the stakeholders in all development activities.

Orissa

The Orissa's past experiences suggest that if the local people equip to handle the first 8 to 10 hours after the flood strikes the losses can be drastically reduced. Trained women in Orissa took responsibility of food and medical supplies to stranded villagers. They collected dry food, rice, bread, jaggery from different houses, packed them, floated the materials to the submerged villages in boats. The women also used rafts made from the trunk of banana tree to transport supplies of kerosene and candles to villagers cut off from the rest of the district. "We experience floods every year and have been responding to it at an individual level. But now we have learnt to respond collectively to a disaster" says SHG member. One can draw lessons from the community that how a community uses local knowledge, skill and resources.

Disaster risk management is the joint initiative of the Government of India and UNDP. The programme which started in 2002, aims at developing the capacity of the local community and panchayati raj institutions for disaster mitigation preparedness and recovery.

In the state of Orissa, after the 1999 Super Cyclone, Government of Orissa's organization OSDMA developed direct contact with district collectors. If there is flood or cyclone OSDMA immediately informed the district collector. The district collectors informed the block development officers. The block development officers contacted village level volunteers. The volunteers included PRI members, school teachers, CBOs, NGOs and they had a special training programme. When the cyclone, SIDR, hit the Bangladesh, the coastal people of Orissa took precautionary measures. The IMD informed the state authorities that the cyclone might hit Orissa. So, the people of coastal districts had a kind of preparedness like procuring extra rations, fuel, match boxes, etc. When the research team visited Jagatsinghpur and Puri district, the cyclone centres, the villagers informed that they had left their homes, to seek refuge in the shelters where the task force members trained by the Red Cross programme stocked supplies of food and drinking water.

In the disaster management team, 30 per cent of women participation was ensured. Government of Orissa with the help of civil society organizations celebrated October 20th as Orissa Disaster Preparedness Day. It started in the year 2000, each year special award given to DMT members. In the Government of Orissa Mission Sakthi Scheme SHGs are trained in construction activities. The Red Cross trained the volunteers and trained the persons involved in searching operations and rescue work. Red Cross also provided training to shelter management and it established shelter management fund. The chairman of the shelter management committee is a Sarpanch.

Awareness Level of Volunteers

Volunteers are aware about the provisions in the Orissa relief code. One of the volunteers said that there was no provision for animal and child care in the Orissa relief code. No provision for pregnant ladies also. They are vulnerables. According to Bharathi Nath, one of the SHG members, women are strong enough to face disasters like cyclone and floods. Now they have well established structure called groups (structural development). Their groups are well functioning. They are ready to lend their services to their members anytime.

SHG members also observed that, there was no coordination between SHGs and Panchayats before the Super Cyclone. Now Panchayati Raj Institution members are ready to collaborate with SHGs, so that everything is possible. SHG members also shared that, they need Panchayat's to help them when problem go beyond their capacity to solve. SHG members actively participate in Palli Sabha and Gram Sabha. Disaster management team was formed by CYSD. Each DMT has 30-40 members. But it is not a continuous process. There is no fund flow for those activities regularly.

Box 17

KHAMUGU

He is the President of the Pani Panchayat. According to him, there is no relationship between Panchayat and DMT. If Panchayat provides materials to DMTs, it is good. Neither Panchayat nor DMT take steps to synergize each other. Disaster management day should be celebrated at Gram Panchayat level. Disaster management should be decentralized process. There should be proper planning at field level and coordination should be there among officials and field level staff. He also stressed that, whatever government formulate, as programme, it is not reaching at village level due to bureaucratic hurdles. There is no coordination among district officials and Sarpanch. Many of the Sarpanches are not aware most of the government schemes.

The study found that after 1999 Super Cyclone, communities were prepared themselves to face any types of disaster. The study found that the communities knew about the issues regarding the disaster preparedness. They informed the study team that the members know about the importance of keeping dry fruits, baby foods, boiling of water before drinking, keeping the valuables in safety, etc. Decisions were taken by the communities. Women participation in community based disaster management programme is more in Orissa than in any other states.

When the villagers heard the news about cyclone on the radio they started following the weather reports. Members of the task force disseminated warning notices through micro phones. Household visits convinced the people to take shelters and helped the most vulnerable people such as the elderly people and pregnant women to the shelters. Biscuits, dry rice, match boxes, batteries for torches were purchased from local shops. Task force members filled the water tank on the roof of the shelters with the drinking water from the nearest tube well and distributed necessary first aid and medicines to the people. This analysis of the information confirms that the community-based strategies implemented by the Orissa Disaster Management programme had been very effective in raising hazard awareness and improving the disaster preparedness.

International agencies working in Orissa formed a group called Inter Agency Group. They regularly met and discussed of the situation in Orissa. They made sure that agencies' work are not duplicated by others. In the recent flood. Diarrhoea spread in Kashyur and Kalahandi districts. It spread from one area to another. This is the fifth time in succession. In the Inter Agency Group meeting, they discussed the long term solutions. They are: (a) How to build capacity in the community? (b) How to reduce breaches? (c) Water and sanitation? (d) Vulnerability map; and (e) Long-term plan. Quality of response is important as there is duplication by every organization in relief activities. Based on the experience, they should come together and work on this specialization. Catholic Relief Services worked on the mobilization of volunteers. Oxfam worked on water and sanitation. Save the Children and UNICEF worked for the welfare of children. Red Cross worked on volunteerism. Help Age India worked for aged people. All International Organizations decided among themselves as to who would be doing what work? To reduce the damages during the disaster, forming local level communities is important and it should be disaster resilient and it should have capacity to take decisions on matters.

SHG members think about forming alternative collectives among themselves. Before 1999 Super Cyclone, women had no chance of thinking about themselves. The SHG members planned for their group members. Before monsoon season, SHG members planned for the safety of the pregnant ladies and infant by ensuring the availability of special food for them. SHG members collected the materials for monsoon season and they collected among themselves and stored them in safer places.

Tamil Nadu

The Government of Tamil Nadu with the help of UNDP implemented disaster management programme. The tsunami in 2004 exposed the vulnerability of women to disaster as more women drowned because they wore *saris* and could not run to safety. They wasted time looking for support from male folk and in finding secure places to keep their money and jewellery. Many of them were dead as they were searching their children.

Besides, gender bias operated during the distribution of relief. In one part—tsunami feedback report, K.M. Ramathal, Chair Person, State Women's Commission, Tamil Nadu, said "women were sidelined and not consulted during the tsunami relief operations. The government officials took down the names of head of the families, mostly men, while handling over relief. These men drank away most of the relief money and women were forced to feed for themselves.

Box 18
Community Participation

DRM programme's real value was exhibited in Samiyarpettai village in Cuddalore district, just two months before the tsunami hit Tamil Nadu's coastal belt in December 2004. The villagers had been trained to face emergency like provide first aid, tying red, yellow and green ribbons on people according to their medical condition, convert doors into stretches, and skilfully rescue persons from unsafe places just two months before the tsunami hit Tamil Nadu's coastal belt in December 2004.

When tsunami hit this village, both men and women tried to put the lessons into practice, compared to the adjoining village of Pudupettai, Samiyarpettai recorded very few deaths and many fisher folk were able to get medical treatment on time because of this training.

Today they are also trained to respond the early warning signs dress accroding to tackle the disaster and swim during the emergency. Block level and district level Disaster Management Committee also formed in schools.

In Tamil Nadu, disaster management committee consists of nine members. But now in many Panchayats, people do not know about the committees. After the formation of the committees by Government order, the committee members attended meetings without the involvement. They attended just for remuneration amount for Rs. 50. In the Vanagiri Panchayat, president sent the committee members for training to Chennai. But there was no women representation in it. In the fisherman community benefits were given by the traditional leaders. People who have society identity card only got benefits. There was no identity card for female headed families. So they were not able to get the benefits. After the intervention of the SHGs, female headed families got identity cards. NGOs didn't concentrate much on this.

Tamil Nadu Tsunami Resource Centre (TNTRC)

Tamil Nadu Tsunami Resource Centre (TNTRC) inaugurated in August 2005 is a joint venture of the United Nations Team for Recovery Support in Tamil Nadu, Catholic Relief Services, Caritas India, Christian Aid, Oxfam, Plan International, Save the Children, World Vision and Support from Government of Tamil Nadu. The TNTRC is a neutral, inclusive and nodal forum at the state level. It is a state level resource centre networking with district resource centres and coordination centres at

Nagapattinam, Kanyakumari, Villupuram, Cuddalore and Thoothukudi and Tirunelveli jointly. It is in the process of setting up district resource centres at Chennai, Kanchipuram and Thiruvallur as well. TNTRC coordinates with the stakeholders in the recovery process to bring about a difference in the lives of the people affected by the tsunami. The overall objective of TNTRC is to facilitate recovery of the tsunami affected communities in a coordinated and equitable way. Another important mandate of TNTRC is collection of and sharing of information and accomplishing it through website, proactive information and the newsletter.

1. Kalpana Chawla Award for Courage and Daring Enterprise for the Year 2005

Success Story

Tmt. Meera, w/o Ramalingam (aged 42 yrs) belongs to Samiyarpettai village in Chidambaram Taluk. She is a member of the "Early-warning Team" under Village Disaster Management Plan and had obtained training in the month of October 2004 as a part of Disaster Risk Management Programme activities to train the villages in handling disasters. On 26th December 2004, at the time of Tsunami, on knowing that the water was entering the village, she boldly rushed to the seashore to do her duty of warning the people who were there, without caring for her own life. There were about five hundred people on the seashore area. Due to her efforts in mobilizing the people to run towards the land, many lives were saved. On seeing the water level further rising, when the second set of waves came, she also ran away but the waves reached her and she could manage to save herself only by clinging to the gate of the house of Pattanichi on the beach road near the sea shore area. Even after having saved herself from the jaws of death, she continued her services with exemplary courage and bravery and saved a few more lives by making efforts to rescue others who were struggling in water. She held the hands of four such persons, namely Aananthan, Mathi, Indra and Subramaniam and dragged them inside the house of Pattanichi. Due to her act of courage and bravery Meera was awarded the Kalpana Chawla Award for Courage and Daring Enterprise for the year 2005-06 with the cash prize of Rs. 5 lakh.

2. Bio-shields like Mangroves completely protected the Panchayat from the Killer waves

Bio-shield

This story is from the village of Thandavarayan Cholan Pettai, Chidambaram Taluk, Cuddalore district, Tamil Nadu. Bio-shields like mangroves were grown in the village with the support and guidance from M.S. Swaminathan Research Foundation. This had completely protected the Panchayat from the killer waves of tsunami on 26th December 2004. Almost similar is the case of Madamedu, a costal village in Sirkali Taluk of Nagapattinam district. The impact of tsunami was very less compared to others in this village because of the growth of Casurina trees on the shores by the Tamil Nadu Forest Department. The stories do not end here. In Nallavedu village near Pondicherry, M.S. Swaminathan Foundation has been running a Village Knowledge Centre having computers, early warning systems, internet connectivity through satellites, etc. Awareness and Warning System were placed at the centre of the village. Every time the Public Address System sounded on 26th December 2004, when the tsunami struck the shores of Indonesia, Mr. Vijaya Kumar a native of the village and the farmer volunteer at the Centre who was at that time working in Singapore heard the tsunami news in Indonesia through Singapore TV. He telephoned the VKC of Nallavedu Village. The centre immediately spread the news through public address system. People were evacuated early enough to avert a major destruction of life.

In Tamil Nadu, a few NGOs worked with community. Others didn't take up the views of the community. Whatever, they were planning to do for relief, rehabilitation activities, they implemented them without the community's involvement. For example, during the construction of houses, all NGOs were target oriented and they gave housing construction activities to contractors. In Kameshwaram Panchayat, houses were already in dilapidated condition. Not only NGOs but Government also lacked faith in the community. They did not have faith in the panchayats also. After tsunami struck, many IAS officers were appointed to look after the relief works. Each IAS officer was in-charge of seven to eight panchayats. In P.R. Puram and Kameshwaram Panchayat, Gram Panchayat presidents mobilized community, youth and others for relief work. When an issue came for the construction of temporary shelter, P.R. Puram panchayat president suggested a place based on his local knowledge. An IAS officer in-charge of this panchayat refused to listen to the Panchayat president's suggestions and she ordered to construct shelter in some other place. This created a problem. During monsoon season, water locked the entire temporary shelter area. Gram Panchayat president faced a problem to drain water from the temporary shelter area. She also listened to the views of the community and panchayat president for the distribution of relief. She ordered the construction of a temporary shelter relying on own knowledge of the local conditions.

Andhra Pradesh

The government structure is very strong in Andhra Pradesh. A few NGOs are now working on community-based disaster preparedness. With the help of NGOs the communities were collecting flood management fund. Wherever NGOs are working with the community, they were responding to the flood situation positively. They claimed their rights. They were collecting relief materials from the Government and distributing them among themselves in an equitable way. A research team visited both the NGOs intervention village and other villages where NGOs were not intervening. The team found that non-NGOs intervened villages were not aware of their claim: How much Government was providing relief and other details? Even though flood causes damages for the life and livelihood of the communities felt that the floods made their land fertile.

Box 19
Livelihood

Livelihood of the people in the rural areas depends only on agriculture. Since so many generations of people use to go to upper lands due to rainy season and stay there. After the rainy season, they use to come back to the village and do farming during the remaining season of the year. Advantage of flood to the farming is that soil became very fertile. Farmers comparatively got very good yield after the floods. That yield is a good relief, for no work during the rainy season.

Gujarat

Firstly, the government extended to the earthquake-affected communities, a range of choices from complete and partial relocation to the sites of reconstruction. Communities through a participatory process of decision-making exercised their option. Selection of a new village site was made with the involvement of the village level Samiti or Gram Sabha of the village and the NGO/Agency involved. A predominant sentiment among the communities for minimal relocation had been a guiding influence on the housing recovery policy. Secondly, in view of heterogeneity and a large geographical spread of settlements in the earthquake-affected region, it was decided to decentralize the housing reconstruction process through the delegation of technical and financial powers to the district administration and Area Development Authorities that were constituted for the urban centres of Kutch. Thirdly, it was primarily a community-based, owner-driven programme, with technical assistance from the engineers provided by the government, building centres, NGOs, etc. Owners organized reconstruction, repairs and strengthened through informal or formal contracts with small contractors, artisans and masons. Finally, the recovery programme was based on a tripartite partnership, involving the Government of Gujarat, the private sector (including NGOs) and the beneficiaries themselves. This partnership harnessed the strengths of each of these participant groups, thus producing a practical and feasible implementation strategy.

In order to involve the communities in the reconstruction programme, the repair of school rooms was entrusted to the village civil work committee. The committee by its active involvement repaired all the 42,678 damaged school rooms in a record time out of 54,898 class rooms. Before rebuilding the house, the NGOs discussed with the engineers and the communities and also keeping in mind the three major disasters, namely earthquake, flood and cyclone, they have structured/ planned the houses. We formed one group, which included one representation from each community. This group received all the relief material and distributed them to the communities. Since, there was representation from each community; we found no problem in the distribution relief materials.

After the earthquake, we got good shelters and some infrastructures such as Teachers quarters, water facilities, electricity and sanitation. The NGOs formed Self Help Groups and promoted the creation of livelihoods. They also gave us training to establish our livelihoods. Apart from the livelihoods training the presidents and ward members, women and youth were trained in Disaster Relief work. But now AIDMI is planning to give training regarding disasters. Also earlier the committee was formed with elders, but now the elders themselves suggested to have the youths in the disaster relief work.

The NGO and the Government involved the communities in building their own houses. This gave mental satisfaction to the communities that they had built their houses as they wished. The constitutional Panchayat president, ward members, traditional leaders and communities were involved in the distribution of relief materials. The strategy might have different from village to village. For example, in some villages the NGOs gave importance to the constitutional Panchayat presidents and ward members because they did not want to form another committee for that at that critical time. Hence, after the earthquake, the period of constitutional Panchayat was over and it was time to form the next Panchayat. Some NGOs formed a group and distributed the relief materials. In some villages, the communities constituted a group, which includes one representatives from each community.

The government assessed the damage into five categories and in categorizing the five, they involved the communities. It was transparent, so the communities felt happy in this process. One NGO was involved in shelter building activities. It collected Rs. 4000 from each beneficiary and created an account for Disaster Management. But the drawback was that the communities did not know how much was collected and deposited. Before rebuilding the houses, the NGOs discussed the plan with the engineers and the communities and also keeping in mind the three major disasters, namely earthquake, flood and cyclone, they structured/planned the houses accordingly. The big farmers provided food grains to the poor people and also at the emergency time they permitted the poor to stay in their own houses.

Community Participation

Availability of funds, commitment of the government and resilience of the people contributed to the success of the programme, the most important factor which made this programme a success was the participation of the people at all stages. The participation of the community was ensured in identifying the problem, arriving at a solution and implementation of the programme. The whole reconstruction and rehabilitation programme was designed and was implemented as a community participation support programme. The decision to relocate or build the houses was taken by the communities themselves in the gram sabha meeting.

Communities were involved not only in housing reconstruction but also in repair and reconstruction of school rooms. More than 180 public consultations were conducted in the four municipal towns of Kutch for town planning and infrastructure reconstruction. As part of the long-term disaster preparedness as a special programme to reduce the economic vulnerability was launched through the Department of Women and Child Development. The approach was to form self-help groups, which involved an income generating activity through NGOs with assured linkages.

Disaster Management Team with the Inclusion of Women and Other Training Activities

In Gujarat, before the earthquake, the state was affected by other disasters like drought and flood. From that time onwards, the community was trained for disaster management. A disaster management team was formed in which both women and men were included. Mock drills in every affected villages were conducted. Sarpanches in the villages were also given training by both NGOs and the government. Some of the communities from Kharadiya gram Panchayat in Kutch District informed that "Now if any disaster occurs they are ready to face the situation". Thus, wherever NGOs and Panchayats had coordination, the community was sensitized in various activities (Tima Village Vaduvan Block, Surendranagar district; Kharadiya gram Panchayat and Thuga, Kutch district; Shargud village in Pathan district).

Listing out what they needed to reduce the impact of recurring disasters, repair of roads and canals were done so that the villages remained connected with the outside world. Clearing of drains that allowed flood waters to drain away, strengthening of fragile houses to ensure safety during disaster were also undertaken.

Community responses were effective in many places. The following few examples show this:

Pre-Disaster Phase Measures: Contrasting Bangladesh and India

Bangladesh had suffered a major cyclone in Cox's Bazar in 1970, which left approximately 5 lakh people dead. But, in early 1990s, when a cyclone of similar intensity hit the country, although the population density of Bangladesh had almost doubled, only, 128 people were killed. This was possible because of the proper implementation of the pre-disaster phase measures in the country. However, in India the pre-disaster phase measures have been found completely missing in many cases. For instance, as has been reported in the media, in the first week after the Gujarat earthquake, there were significantly high number of surgeons in the earthquake hit regions. But they could not conduct surgery because of lack of equipment and electricity. Telecom lines were all defunct. So difficulty arose in transmission of much needed information about the need, type and location of relief work. Even though Kutch (the worst hit district in the earthquake) belongs to one of those seismic zones in India, which faces the highest risk of earthquake, the government apparatus was got completely unprepared for the disaster.

People-centred Approach to Disaster Risk Reduction: A Few Examples

In Bangladesh, local communities in the disaster prone areas came up with ways to protect the vulnerable people from floods and cyclones. The villagers used colour coded flags for evacuation, yellow means get ready and red means leave your houses now. Instructions were broadcast over loud speakers mounted on mosque for prayers and in temples, bells were rung in special ways to indicate the approaching danger.

A user-friendly computer aided rating system to warn people of fire dangers has been quite successful in Namibia. Based on a simple analysis of rainfalls levels, the system warns the local communities about impending wild fire hazards which doesn't require especially fancy technologies or expensive telecommunication systems.

In Bihar, India, there have been instances of villages arranging themselves into teams to tackle floods. One group of villagers monitored water levels, another took care of vulnerable people's homes, while a third team carried the injured to a higher ground. A fourth team cleared the village of snakes and dirty water when it was time for people to return to their houses.

During floods in Assam, people used to communicate flood situation through a tall bamboo tied with flags at its top. If one red colour flag is tied with bamboo this is indication of "Flood is likely to come". The two flags tied are indication of "flood is already occurred and be prepared" and three flags are indication of "vacating village immediately with essential survival kits (contents of two day's food for the family)".

As per the 2005 Disaster Management Act, all four states have worked for the disaster management by forming the committees. But following problems remain in institutionalizing the committees. The committee members did not get training regularly. In Sammiyarpettai Panchayat in Tamil Nadu most of the committee members migrated abroad. In Orissa, the committee members lacked financial support. Andhra Pradesh government was not actively involving in forming committees. This could be avoided by integrating the committees into panchayats.

To sum up, wherever community was empowered, it has taken a lead role in disaster preparedness and management. In the recent disaster in Tamil Nadu, Andhra Pradesh, Orissa, Gujarat communities managed themselves during the first two days. After the intervention of the NGOs and Government, the attitude of the community changed. After 1999 Super Cyclone, the Government of Orissa took a number of measures with the help of UNDP and Red Cross. But community-based Disaster Management Programme has not been yet institutionalized. In the districts of Puri and Jagatsinghpur of Orissa, Disaster Management Teams were formed and people were trained in all the villages. But there was no follow up. UNDP is providing very minimum financial support to each of the Disaster Management Team. That amount is not sufficient. The DMT does not have linkages with Gram Panchayat. Gram Panchayat is a well-established institution at the grassroots level based especially on the 73rd Constitutional Amendment Act. Creating DMT without the knowledge of Gram Panchayat and without linking them with Gram Panchayat doesn't give desired results. In Andhra Pradesh Government structures are very strong. Gram Panchayats and communities have very limited role to play. Distribution of relief is done through Revenue Officials. Communities are satisfied once their loss of properties are noted by the Revenue Officials. They are not bothering whether they are getting proper compensation or not. NGOs lack perspective on grassroots governance. They are working in a very sporadic way. NGOs consider village as a basic unit, not panchayats.

5

Role of Panchayats in Disaster Management and Interface between Traditional Panchayats and the Constitutional Panchayats

PART I : ROLE OF PANCHAYATS IN DISASTER MANAGEMENT

Panchayats and Municipalities as local governing institutions have a constitutional mandate under the 73rd and 74th Constitutional Amendments Act. Subsequent to the 73rd Constitutional Amendment Act, all four states have passed the confirmative act. For the first time women, Dalits and Adivasis were elected as leaders of local body institutions. Past studies show that if the capacities of the local bodies institutions developed through training, they can work more efficiently and in a participatory way with accountability and transparency. Good governance can be an instrumental feature in poverty reduction. The Articles 243G of the Constitution visualizes Panchayats as institutions of self- governance. A comprehensive list of 29 subjects have been provided to the Panchayats through 11th Schedule. The success of the Panchayats depends upon the devolution of powers, functions and functionaries. This study conducted a few intensive case studies with select Panchayat Presidents to find out the role played by them in the recent disasters in the four states.

Orissa

Orissa has three-tier Panchayat Raj System, namely District Panchayat, Block Panchayat and Gram Panchayat. Instead of Gram Sabha, Orissa has got Palli Sabha. Apart from the implementation of Development programmes, the panchayat system has the following roles with regard to disaster management.

In the state of Orissa, the village level disaster management committee is headed by ward members of gram Panchayat. The gram Panchayat level disaster management committee is headed by the gram Panchayat President. The Chairman of the Panchayat Samiti will chair the block level disaster management committee. District level disaster management committee is headed by the District Collector.

With regard to PRI functionaries, they involve in CCP planning from the beginning, they involve in joint monitoring, relief distribution and management. Involvement of PRI functionaries in the advocacy is considered more important. Community-based river embankment protection is in practice. Involving PRIs in life and non-life insurance is also considered important.

Mr. Rangalal Jamuda, Commissioner and Secretary, Revenue Department, Orissa emphasized that the role of Panchayat institutions is crucial and needs to be integrated with the disaster management processes. He also cautioned about the negative role of groups/individuals during disaster in terms of spreading incorrect information and advised for devising ways to counter these. He emphasized on the training aspect of volunteers and other disaster management workforce.

He further said that Panchayat should be actively involved in Disaster preparedness, relief distribution and rehabilitation activities. PRIs should be empowered to address time gaps between relief and rehabilitation activities. Community-based disaster preparedness has to be done by the panchayats.

Role of Civil Society/PRIs in Community Preparedness

Following are the activities of the panchayats in association with civil society organizations:

(a) Upgradation of contingency plans regularly,
(b) Providing capacity building to task force regularly by the panchayat,
(c) Providing resources to task forces,
(d) Keeping rescue equipments and survival kits ready,
(e) Safe storage of essential commodities and materials for construction of temporary shelters should be ready,
(f) Feeding cattle's, medicine and water,
(g) Providing food to the task force in time,

(h) Restoration of infrastructure,

(i) They have to link CCP programmes with existing development programmes. They have to provide basic services. Coordination and networking is more important. They have to conduct awareness camps regularly.

Issues

They have to sustain the interest of the trained volunteers, and keep their motivational level high. They have to institutionalize the contingency plan. They must dovetail the development plans to vulnerability reduction and mitigation measures.

With regard to Panchayati Raj Institutions, Government of Orissa has framed detailed guidelines. Government of Orissa has delegated 29 powers in 77 subjects. At the block level CBTs were formed. It works in proactive manner. It was formed prior to 99 Super Cyclone also. But it concentrated as preparedness in the sense of awareness in the year 2000. NGO followed the community-based disaster mitigation programme from the year 2000. Before that it was defunct. As far as Orissa government is concerned, it planned to provide awareness programmes on Tsunami in 328 villages. In those programmes, it encouraged and ensured that the involvement of ward members. Apart from the ward members, Sarpanch, Panchayat Samiti and District Panchayat members and Chairman were targeted to give capacity building for disaster preparedness.

Gram Panchayat can provide assistance to families who do not belong to the particular Panchayats. Gram Panchayat Presidents need not get approval from the BDOs for providing assistance to such families.

Role of Panchayats in Cyclone Shelter Maintenance

Government of Orissa has constructed 99 multi-purpose cyclone shelters. Sarpanches were the integral part of the cyclone centres from the construction to maintenance of the cyclone shelters. Government of Orissa is following decentralized disaster management system. The Sarpanches have financial devolution power also. Sarpanches are not only acting during the disaster time by way of distributing relief materials, they also acted as facilitators. The house building assistance to the beneficiaries should be distributed through the Sarpanches. Relief should be distributed within 10 days. Destitute families should be given special assistance.

In the government of Orissa, Disaster Management Plan has to be prepared by the Panchayati Raj Institutions. It is the duty of the Panchayati Raj Institutions to watch the flood situation. It has to prepare disaster management plans by including the following details:

(a) Number of disabled,
(b) Low lying areas,
(c) Evacuation plan,
(d) Number of widows,
(e) Women headed families,
(f) Government structures,
(g) Government godowns,
(h) Food stock.

Government of Orissa Initiative

The Government of Orissa realized the importance of training programmes. It started providing training to local body leaders. In the capacity building exercise, changing the attitude of the leaders is important. They realized the importance of including disaster management plan into regular plans. People's representatives also were trained on the entitlements of the people. People's representatives should function as good facilitators. They should be trained on quicker disbursement of material. The government of Orissa prepared a manual for training the Panchayati Raj leaders with Action AID India.

According to Gyan Dass, Panchayati Raj Institutions are in vulnerable conditions. Are we adding existing vulnerability or reducing vulnerability? So many agencies are doing developmental activities, but all activities are not properly coordinated and integrated. Instead of reducing vulnerability, a few agency's activities have increased the vulnerability.

In Orissa PRIs are the well established institutional structure. It is a major stake holder. It is neither insulated nor is it isolated. No substitute for Panchayati Raj Institutions. In case of Panchayati Raj Institution leaders working in relation between PRI leader and government officers are important. Panchayati Raj Institutions have commitments and they have their own agenda. But in reality, effective functioning of Panchayati Raj Institutions depend upon government officers. Attitude of the BDOs should be changed into proactive behaviour. Panchayati Raj Institutions, members get best results from Panchayati Raj leaders.

According to the Second State Finance Commission report of Orissa, it has asked the state government to allocate Rs. 25,000 to each Panchayat as contingency fund that can be used during disasters. It gave lots of recommendations to the government. But the Government did not act upon them. In the state of Orissa, Panchayats are implementing only State and Central government schemes, and they don't have untied funds. The Second State Finance Commission of Orissa has asked the government to provide Rs. 1.0 lakh untied funds to each Panchayat in Orissa, Panchayat Samiti and Zilla Parishad do not have power to impose taxes.

Very few Non-Governmental Organizations have realized the importance of Panchayati Raj Institutions and they are closely working with them. Others have negative opinion about the Panchayati Raj Institutions.

Ramakanthi Singh, Coordinator, Vikas NGO

Vikas NGO integrated all Panchayati Raj Institution members with all their activities from relief to reconstruction. Gradually more importance was given to Panchayati Raj Institution members. Panchayati Raj Institution members should be regularly given (a) Periodical Training, (b) Suggestions for improvement, (c) Creating Awareness, and (d) Keeping health for both human and cattle. While doing reconstruction, a few Panchayati Raj Institution members were given trouble to NGOs because of their party affiliations. Panchayati Raj Institutions have severe financial constraints.

In Korapat—a village committee was formed by the Vikas for the livelihood activities. Without the Panchayat Raj members' consent, no committee was formed by Vikas. Now Panchayati Raj Institution members are coming forward for reconstruction activities. Suggestions were got from the Panchayati Raj Institution members. A Citizen's Forum was also formed in the tribal area and its memorandum was submitted to the government. River embankments were the major works done by the Vikas. Korapat and Kothanal are the very backward districts in Orissa. The Vikas provided training to PRIs, government officials on their role and responsibilities. PRIs need more capacity building training.

According to Krishna Priya Biswal, Vice-Chairman, Panchayat Samiti, Raghunathpur Panchayat's representatives prime responsibilities are to save the people and to clear the road to reach relief materials in time to the villagers. Panchayat representatives played a fair role in distributing relief materials. The Government provided relief materials but they are not sufficient. It provided relief materials equally to all wards. But population varies from ward to ward. Keeping dry fruits in each and every family is important. She also emphasized that only the neighbours were helpful during disasters. In each ward, small groups could be formed and NGOs and governments can provide training to these groups.

She also stressed that each block should be divided into zones. Officers should be appointed for each zone. This will facilitate the smooth functioning of relief activities. She also emphasized more on preparedness than on response. Panchayati Raj Institution members should be aware of the Orissa relief code, government schemes and projects.

According to Debashis Tripathy, Chairman, Raghunathpur Block, ensuring the availability of relief materials and informing all government officials are the prime responsibilities of the elected representatives. Each Gram Panchayat and Panchayat Samiti should start preparing plan at their level. In that planning, identifying existing resources and preparing inventory are essential.

He also emphasized that while constructing roads, elected representatives have to make sure that, they will not wash away in the flood by ensuring that the roads should be laid higher than ground level. The Vice-Chairman of the Raghunathpur Block stressed that, elected representatives need role clarity. Training should be given for all levels of representatives. Ensuring proper coordination among the three tiers of panchayats is important. A few district collectors are cooperative and they closely work with the Panchayats. All Collectors do not have the perception and mind-set needed for cooperative efforts.

According to the Chairman, District Panchayat, Jagatsinghpur, Officials are keeping all Government Schemes as secrets. Regular and continuous capacity building is needed for the elected representatives. He stated that, in the state of Orissa, the quality of Bureaucracies is questionable. After the 1999 Super Cyclone, the Government is not in a position to help people. Whereas the Government of Maharashtra, Delhi, other State Governments responded immediately. The Coastal areas of Orissa are habitually flood-prone areas. Strengthening of river basin is more important. Orissa's Coastal areas are affected by cyclones every year. According to the District Panchayat Chairman, the Panchayat Raj System in Orissa is not synergized with regular Government system. If representatives are not trained, they are not likely to educate the rural masses. Even though the Government of Orissa has long term plans for disaster and they are implemented through the District Administration. The District Panchayat is not aware of the plans. In Orissa there is a well established local governance system. The lack of facilitation among the three tiers make PRIs dysfunctional. He also stressed that there is a lack of facilities like electricity, fuel and toilets at the village level, but the Government is not concentrating on improving basic amenities at village level. The District Collectors have to convene natural calamity meetings once in three months. But they are not serious about this. Meeting is only on the paper. Systematic steps should be taken to prepare permanent plans.

The 73rd Constitutional Amendment Act provided opportunities for PRIs to work efficiently at grassroots to bring changes. But the state government is not giving power to the PRIs. The Government of Orissa have full administrative control over PRIs. Government of Orissa has delegated powers to the Zilla Panchayats in 27 subjects. Still today Zilla Panchayats do not act upon it. The Zilla Panchayat of Jagatsinghpur gave suggestions to the District Administrations regarding strengthening of embankment of river Kattori, a Tributary of Mahanadi. According to the Chairman of the Zilla Parishad four villages are going to be submerged but the district administration is not listening to it.

Problems faced by the Panchayats in and during disasters

1. Problems in distributing relief materials and preparing lists of participants.
2. Construction of storage rooms for the storage of stock.
3. Lack of training on the PRI representatives' roles and responsibilities with regard to Disaster management.
4. Multipurpose cyclone centres—they are under construction through SSA funds, but most of the godowns are constructed in low lying areas and while constructing godowns officials did not consult the PRIs and people.
5. Non-availability of cyclone centres in many panchayats.
6. Non-availability of health facilities, e.g. Rani Kola panchayat, the government hospital is 35 km away from the panchayat. There is only one health centre. Even for the delivery cases they have to go to Jagatsinghpur.
7. District Collectors do not invite the Gram Panchayat leaders for disaster committee meetings.
8. Availability of limited funds for disaster management.

9. Lack of awareness on environmental issues among the Panchayati Raj Institution members. Creation of awareness among Panchayati Raj Institution members on rising the embankment level and improving infrastructural facilities are very difficult and so the disaster mitigation programmes suffer.

Tamil Nadu

The Tamil Nadu Panchayats Act, 1994 is an act to repeal the Madras Panchayats Act, 1958, for establishing a three-tier panchayat raj system in keeping with the Seventy-third Amendment Act, 1992. It relates to the panchayats for greater participation of the people so as to make these institutions of self-government more effective in the implementation of rural development programmes. The Tamil Nadu Panchayat Act provides for preparation and implementation of District development plans. Plan preparation is enforced from the panchayat level. Panchayat union, Panchayat council, village Panchayat, town Panchayat, municipal councils and the municipal corporations work towards overall development plans. District Planning Committee is responsible for the overall coordination of plan preparation. With regard to disaster management, the panchayat raj system in Tamil Nadu has certain provisions. In general, the gram panchayats have duty to provide water, sanitation, road and other basic amenities. But the act provides for avoidance of encroachment of public lands and protection of roadside properties (including trees) belonging to the respective government departments.

Housing

- All housing projects proposed in areas, which are under the jurisdiction of the town or village panchayats, should obtain their clearance/permission. The line department should ensure that this is obtained.
- All construction camps (including plant and equipment) in areas, which are under the jurisdiction of the town or village panchayats, should be established only after obtaining their clearance/permission.

Small Public Works

- All small works proposed in areas, which are under the jurisdiction of the town or village panchayats, should obtain their clearance/permission.

Fisheries

- All workshops, e.g. boat repair yards, which are under the jurisdiction of the town or village panchayats, should be established only after obtaining their clearance/permission.

After Tsunami struck in the coastal districts of Tamil Nadu, many Gram Panchayat presidents took initiatives to bring back normalcy in their areas. The research team conducted intensive case studies with the Gram Panchayat Presidents to document their activities when tsunami struck.

The Villagers Ran towards the Bamboo Bridge Over the Flooded River to Escape from the Chasing Waves

Manimaran, then President of Manikka Pangu Panchayat, said that ensuring the timely distribution of water supply is one of the important tasks the Village Panchayat administration was expected to do. On 26th December, Manimaran woke up early morning and proceeded to switch on the power pump—OHT water supply system. Though there was an operator to do this, Manimaran did not wait for him. Then, as usual, he went to his fields. Near the field there was a tea-stall and in front of the tea-stall there was a pond. Passersby crowded round it and saw that the water in the pond rose up and down around 8.45 a.m.

He then returned home. The houses of the fishermen were located within 200 metres of the seashore. When he was returning, there was a sound of alarm. He saw waves from the sea rise up to 10 metres and the water was very thick and dark. Thorny bushes, thatches, broken logs, debris of damaged houses and other buildings all rolled on along the flood water. He immediately shouted at his sons and his wife to run away from the house. He got into his house and brought out his bike and drove to the nearby power plant office to contact the District Collectorate. He came to know that the Collector was already out to attend to the call of the public in this regard. Hence, he drove back on his bike to the habitation against the flood water but could not proceed. He fell down in the speedy flow of water and he was able to hold on to a tree and thus escaped. The villagers ran towards the bamboo bridge over the flooded river to escape from the chasing waves. Though the water was up to the level of the bamboo bridge, the bridge was strong enough for them to cross over. It was so fortunate that just four days back, the bamboo bridge had been repaired. Otherwise, there would have been no way to escape, Manimaran said.

Immediate Action with Community and the Existing Bamboo Bridge Saved number of People from the Killer Waves

Manimaran, with the help of other villagers, enabled others to climb over the bridge and to cross over to the other side, one by one. The youth of Anaikoil Village, which is a non-fishermen village, rushed immediately and helped the children and the old to escape. In the meantime, the thorny bushes and debris struck against the bamboo bridge and it was later found that there were two dead bodies of children. The corpse of the children were removed and then Manimaran, with others, visited the habitation where they found dead bodies of children and adults. The dead bodies were removed by all and kept at the side of the local temple. Till 4 O'clock in the evening the rescue operation and removal of dead bodies was attended to, Manimaran said. After 4.00 p.m., he thought about his sons and wife. Immediately, he visited Thirukadaiyur temple where all the people were staying. On his way, he was told that only one of his sons was seen. He is heart beat rose. With the hope that his family members would be alive, he moved towards Anaikulam near Thirukadaiyur, i.e., 7 km from Manickappangu. He found his two sons and his wife there. Immediately, he returned to his habitation in Manickappangu and engaged in burial activities.

After Alerting the Fishermen Community in the Seashore about the Killer Waves, She Sought Help from Officials at the Police Station

Selvi Manimegalai is the President of Cauvery Poompattinam Village Panchayat of Kollidam Panchayat Union. She belongs to the fishermen community. She is unmarried. Even at the age of 50 years, she moves fast at the call of the public. The interview was interrupted due to the visit of the revenue officials who came over to the village with regard to the complaint of Selvi Manimegalai against an encroacher. She just sat on a two wheeler behind the driver and urged him to drive quickly to the spot. It was only after half an hour that she returned and resumed the interview.

Selvi Manimegalai recollected the worst day, December 26, 2004. On that day she was watching the TV around 7.30 a.m. and the news about the tsunami hit in Indonesia was flashed. She immediately rushed outside and ran to Chinakuttai (small pond) to check for the consequences in the village. Manimegalai informed that during the Gujarat earthquake, there was a sensation of body movement in Cauvery Poompattinam. Hence, on December 26 after viewing the TV news, she went to the pond side and witnessed that the water in the pond had risen up to two feet and there were bubbles. To alert the villagers, she ran to the seashore where the habitation of the fishermen community was located. Immediately, she telephoned to the higher officials from the police station. In the mean time, the sea water had rushed to the shore and within fifteen minutes the water rose to neck level. Children were struggling in the flood and were saved by youths. The walls of houses broke down and the flood water forcibly drew away everything around the habitation.

Earlier six huts had been constructed in the area by the community to house a few larger families. Just three days earlier, Manimegalai had evicted all the inhabitants of the six huts and removed the thorny bushes/ trees and cleared the approaches to all the roads leading to the shore-habitations. When the tsunami waves hit on that day, it was through that passage the community members ran fast and escaped from the attack of the killer waves. But mostly women and children who could not run quickly became victims. Manimegalai shared her experiences with tears in her eyes.

It is Heartening that People from Various Other Parts of the Village and Nearby Village Volunteered Themselves and Rendered Great Service to the Affected

The northern side of Cauvery Poompattinam is the China Cauvery Pattinam where about 300 huts are located near the sea. Here 87 deaths occurred, Manimegalai said. She telephoned to various government departments and the District Collector. In the meantime, the Block Development Officials came to the villages and facilitated the relief works. The fishermen community handled the removal and burial of dead bodies. Several bodies lay under collapsed buildings and constructions. A JCB machine was brought to remove the debris and the dead bodies were recovered, Manimegalai said. The Village Panchayat administration arranged for refreshments to the community members. Biscuit and milk were provided. Lunch was also given by the Village Panchayat administration. The non-fishermen community of Manthekarai volunteered for relief activities. The nearby villagers of Mangamadam and the merchants and traders of Sirkali town came over and distributed food packets, Manimegalai explained.

Manimegalai said that the life of the fishermen community was very peaceful and joyful. They used to lie down on the shore fearlessly and allowed their little children to run about and play on the shore. At the age of twelve years, the boys used to accompany their fathers and happily ventured into the sea. Steadily they learned the life style, customs and techniques of life on the sea. The boys became full time bread winners of their family at the age of seventeen or eighteen and would get one share of the fishes collected at sea. In the fishing trade, there is no master-servant relationship. It is mere sharing of catches based on a basic rule. Whatever they get they share it. They enjoy their life with what they have. Their life is always entwined with nature.

They spent about one month at temples/schools, temporary shelters. The role of NGOs in this was noteworthy, Manimegalai said. The killer waves destroyed everything, they lost their near and dear ones, houses and other properties. It was a total loss, Manimegalai felt. It was only in the past two or three decades that the life of fishermen had taken the path of progress and prosperity owing to science and technology, Manimegalai said. Due to the availability of boats and variety of nets, oil engine, and their consolidation as a sangam and the cooperative venture in fishing that their income was high. Hence, their comforts and enjoyments increased. But due to the tsunami everything was destroyed.

The life in the temporary shelter was a horrible and their loss was very pitiable. The Village Panchayat administration took steps to provide protected water supply, build roads, remove debris and clean roads and passages, protect environmental sanitation, health of women, immunize children and persuade the government to identify a suitable site to relocate the affected houses, Manimegalai explained. Manimegalai expressed gratitude to the services and assistance rendered by the government and non-governmental organizations. But she felt sorry for their attitude towards the community. Instead of discussing with the community to identify the felt needs among the youths and children and other stakeholders of the community, the NGO staff just provided what they chose. For instance, to a child of a victim family was given four bags from four different NGOs, but nobody bothered to find out what could be kept inside the bags. People wanted more interaction from the people who came from outside. But people who came here distributed material and took photographs and disappeared. Donors and the government provided material relief but not psychological relief. This is the feeling of the community.

She suggested that there should be a disaster management committee at the village level, Panchayat level and taluk level in the coastal areas. She was of the opinion that farmers and farm labourers should also be compensated from the government relief packages and NGO assistance. It is the whole coastal economy, environment and the sustainable livelihood which were affected. Hence, development should be holistic covering all stakeholders, Manimegalai reiterated.

Prathabaramapuram is a village Panchayat located near the Velankanni Church. Seruthur is a fishermen community village under the jurisdiction of *Prathabaramapuram Village Panchayat. The President, Sri R.V. Swaminathan,* explained the details of the relief activities undertaken by his Village Panchayat administration.

With the Help of the Private Transport Companies, and Village Youths, Evacuation of the People from the Coastal Area to the Safer Places

The President, hearing the news of the tsunami from the local community, informed the Police, Fire Station, RDO and the District Collector over the phone. Since he is a well informed person, he had all the phone numbers. He made arrangements to move the affected people to the hospitals. At the same time, all the families from the coastal area came out and fled to safer places. The President helped them to go over to safer places, far away from the coastal area, by making arrangements with private transport companies, lorry and tractor owners. He found it very difficult to bring transport to this village. Most of them were accommodated in marriage halls and schools located in the village itself. The President arranged for preparing breakfast and lunch with the help of local community volunteers.

In the meantime, he made arrangements for visiting Seruthur Village. A team of youths and other volunteers from the main village

Prathabaramapuram joined the youth and elders of the fishermen community. They started the identification of dead bodies, and removed them for burial. In the meantime government officials started to go over the affected area and collected various details and the President assisted them by providing the necessary details through verification and clarification from the concerned families and the community. The Panchayat President established his control over the entire activities and left no room for government officials to act on their own. In the beginning he did not wait for the arrival of the officials.

NGOs Sought the Help of the Constitutional Panchayat President for the Smooth Distribution of Relief Materials

The second and third day after the disaster, a number of NGOs came to the site and distributed various items of relief materials. The President helped them to identify the victim families and assisted in proper distribution of relief materials to the concerned families. By then the Government formed a team of various sectoral officials and the relief work was systematized—removal of debris, restoration of electricity, drinking water supply, link road and connectivity to the affected area. The President joined the official team and assisted them. At the camp site, medical check-up and medicines were also provided by the team.

Various NGOs, volunteers and social institutions visited and a lot of activities were undertaken by them like counselling, distribution of provisions, play materials and other essential materials like blankets, buckets, vessels etc. to the affected families. In general, the NGOs met the President and sought the help of the Panchayat Administration to contact the right persons or community leaders. Without any confusion the relief activities were properly carried out. The President informed that some NGOs, when they directly contacted the affected families, faced a lot of problems in distributing the materials. The presence of the Village Panchayat President brought some order, Swaminathan claimed. Further the President helped in identifying and establishing a temporary shelter with necessary facilities like drinking water supply and toilet and electricity connection.

When the Government arranged the dole and other cash benefits to the affected families, the President assisted the Village Administrative Officer in listing the eligible families in this regard. He gave an impression to the officials as well as the members of the community that he is a person with leadership qualities and with a sense of commitment. He maintained the exact data with regard to deaths and damages to properties. He did not permit anyone to take advantage of their misery. He demonstrated his leadership in managing the situation very effectively. In many places the communities were divided on caste lines for distribution of relief material. But in his Panchayat he maintained harmony among the various segments of the society.

The President of Prathabaramapuram Panchayat assisted the local NGO engaged by The Hunger Project, Gandhigram Rural Institute, to carry out the Micro Planning exercise. He assisted in identifying the local volunteers, farmer groups and SHG groups, helped in the baseline survey, focused group discussion, in conducting PRA exercise, and drafting the developmental plan for the Village Panchayat. Swaminathan explained that generally the fishermen community was very traditional in nature: they used to come to the Village Panchayat to stake their entitlements, namely drinking water, road, street lights etc. For other needs, they used to seek the help of the traditional Panchayat leaders. But tsunami created a new atmosphere and interface with all sections of the community, Swaminathan said. It is a normal tendency among the poor, whether they are affected or not, where there is any opportunity to get any assistance from the government, they utilize it by any means. This is being exploited by all from politicians to officials. This, in fact, created a whole lot of problems in the communities. But Panchayat leaders, with their responsible action could avoid many of the unpleasant situations. The elected Panchayat leaders had to discharge their duties with a sense of commitment.

Immediately the Victims of the Killer Waves were Injected with TT

Kanakasundaram, President of Kameshwaram Panchayat, attended a training programme on Disaster Management in the State Institute of Rural Development, one week before the occurrence of the tsunami. He learnt how to manage a disaster in the training. On the day of the tsunami, he informed the local police, Revenue Divisional Officer immediately; then he contacted his own party men (Communist Party of India-Marxist) and requested them to send vehicles. He transported all the affected to the nearby Panchayat. As he maintained good rapport with other Panchayat Presidents, Thirupoondi West Panchayat President accommodated the affected persons in a Marriage Hall and arranged for food.

The President, with the help of youngsters, evacuated the injured persons and they sent them to the Thirupoondi hospital. The President also contacted local hospitals and doctors rushed to the Kameshwaram Panchayat. All the injured persons were injected with TT by the nurses on the third day. After settling the affected persons and evacuating the non-affected persons to the nearby safety area, he rushed to the seashore with youngsters and started collecting the dead bodies. All the collected dead bodies were put in one place and he took a photograph of them. He informed the District Collector that the bodies were in a bad condition and so they could not do post-mortem and they were going to bury the dead bodies. He arranged refreshments for the doctors also.

On the second and third day after the tsunami occurrence, NGOs helped Panchayats in relief and rehabilitation activities. NGOs took census from each hamlet. They cleaned the villages with the help of volunteers. They provided rice and *dal* for all the affected. They provided psycho-social comfort. They helped the fishermen community to restore their livelihoods. They gave fishnets, shelters; they even provided mineral water for 3 months in Chinoor Pudhupettai. Initially NGOs had not even asked any document or identification for providing the houses in Chinoor Pudhupettai of Cuddalore district.

NGOs Played a Major Role not only in Relief Activities but also in the Rehabilitation and Restoring Livelihood Process of the Affected People

NGOs like ASSEFA, SEVALAYA started child care centres in the Panchayats for pre-school going children and tuition for school going children. Apart from school subjects, subjects like child rights, non-violence, *yoga*, Kutti Doctor and Balar Panchayat. The committee members learnt about their roles, and the responsibilities. All the NGOs had display board to show their transparency. Initially the district collectors discussed with the affected and now NGOs represented the affected people. For all above said activities NGOs were closely working with Gram Panchayat.

In general, the NGOs used to meet the President and sought the help of the Panchayat administration to contact the right persons or community leaders. The President of Prathabaramapuram Panchayat informed that some NGOs, when they directly contacted the affected families faced a lot of problems in managing the materials. In Chinoor Pudhupettai, all officials, NGOs, MLAs and MPs, party leaders directly went to the fishermen area and distributed directly; they did not think of consulting the ward members and Panchayat Presidents.

In Prathabaramapuram, the Gram Panchayat Presidents requested all Non-governmental organizations to submit their accounts in the Gram Sabha, many did not listen to the Panchayat President. It shows that the NGOs do not have faith in running their organization transparently. But, according to V.S. Prabakaran, ASSEFA, NGOs asked the Panchayat Presidents to involve in their activities. ASSEFA had discussion with Gram Panchayat President then they started their activities. The village Panchayat President cooperated with the NGOs. But the Panchayat President always expected money from the NGOs and they even demanded Rs. 1.0 lakh from the NGOs. Many NGOs constructed temporary shelters with tin sheets instead of coconut leaves. This created health problem to the inmates.

Many NGOs did not take Panchayat as the lowest level of administrative unit and formed Disaster management committee at the hamlet level. They argued that hamlets are scattered. It is impossible to strengthen the disaster management committee at the Panchayat level. But the Panchayats monitored hamlet level disaster management committee and strengthened it.

According to the Prathabaramapuram Panchayat President, when the government arranged the dole and other cash benefits to the affected families, the President assisted the village Administrative officer in choosing the eligible families. He gave an impression to the officials as well as the members of the community that he was a person with leadership and a sense of commitment. He maintained exact data with regard to the deaths and damages to the properties. He did not permit anyone to take advantage of their misery. He demonstrated his leadership qualities in managing the situation very effectively. In many places the communities were divided on caste lines for distribution of relief material. But in Prathabaramapuram Panchayat, the President maintained harmony among the various segments of the society.

Gender Sensitivity in all Her Activities

Vairakannu, the then president of Vanagiri Panchayat took efforts to restore his panchayat from disaster when tsunami struck that panchayat. People were coming towards Dharmavasal and Kuruvi. Kuruvi is ten kilometres away from Vanagiri. In the Vanagiri panchayat fire woods were kept on both sides of the villages which caused a huge loss of lives. There were 47 deaths in Vanagiri panchayats. Out of this 19 female, 6 male, 12 male children and 10 female children. When Tsunami struck, the President was inside her house. In the beginning, she didn't realize the magnitude of the loss. After hearing and seeing the loss of lives and property, she acted very quickly. She found many dead bodies naked. She immediately provided *sarees* and *dothies* to cover the dead bodies. She arranged for shrouds to cover the dead bodies. By evening she found 26 dead bodies, she collected them all and put them in one place. After getting proper permission from the police and relatives, she arranged for the burial. The Panchayat President arranged food with the help of NGOs and other caste people. In the mean time, she collected all dead bodies for burial. The Village Administrative Office in this panchayat was very lethargic and he didn't properly cooperated with the panchayat for relief activities. She arranged token system for the distribution of relief materials. Still the conflict arose because traditional leaders misused the relief materials. To sort out this problem, the District Collector encouraged the youths to involve in distributing the relief materials. But this led to a conflict which necessitated the intervention of the police. Now the case is pending in the court.

In Vanagiri panchayat in the first beneficiary list the schedule caste people were not included. The second list was prepared by including them. But this was rejected by the traditional leaders. Later they accepted that list, but the community did not accept the list.

The panchayat demanded 750 houses, the NGOs gave 300 houses and government accepted to construct the rest with a condition that people should have house tax receipts with them. So, the president provided house tax receipts to all on that day itself, even for the people who did not own house.

Attitude of NGOs: NGOs lack faith in the local body leaders. They didn't discuss with presidents regarding the benefits. This led to conflicts in many panchayats. For the construction of houses, NGOs appointed contractors without the panchayat's consultation. The NGO named HOPE was cheated by the contractor for an amount of Rs. 12 lakhs.

Conflict: This village Panchayat has seven hamlets, among them four hamlets received relief materials, the rest of the hamlets did not receive any benefits. Without understanding the scenario, they blamed the Panchayat President. All the community leaders helped voluntarily at the initial stage of Tsunami. After somedays, when the NGOs and government started to dump the materials and money to the affected people, their attitude changed. Their interest went towards money and materials. The government refused to provide a house to a person who was living beyond 200 metres from the sea (i.e., he is living around 600 metres) and the house was not damaged heavily. But the government sanctioned a house to a person who lived 3 kms away from the sea. The government acted with some logic which was not understandable to the common people.

Transparency: The Panchayat issued the relief materials by announcing the names in mike in loud speaker. But when traditional panchayat took charge, everything was kept as a secret, so the problem increased. They prepared a list in which 24 families were removed, that also created more problems in the village. Because of these problems, still in this village no one took steps to erect pillar in memory of the dead due to Tsunami. So to avoid this type of situation, transparency is needed at all level.

Observation by the Panchayat Presidents

- The victims of Tsunami belonged to below poverty line but above poverty line families got benefits when compared to the former.
- The thorny fire wood trees were the main reason for a number of deaths.

K. Kumari Kaliyaperumal, Vanagiri Panchayat

- She blamed the card system of distributing the relief materials. She directly blamed the Village Administrative Officer, the president and the traditional leaders who took 10-20 cards at an average and took advantage of those cards.
- She also blamed the NGOs' steps related to construction activities. The building is in a bad shape and the doors they fixed for the houses were of bad quality.
- She was the first to form self help groups in the village in 1997. Since Self Help Group Movement was not familiar at that time, the traditional leaders won't allow her to attend the social functions. Now, especially after Tsunami, the number of SHGs increased more than 160. In the recent election she was asked to contest for the presidentship of the panchayat by the traditional leaders themselves.

Formation of Disaster Management Committee before Tsunami Struck was with True Spirit

Gnanaprakasam, President of Leepuram Panchayat, has won many accolades as the Panchayat President. He won the Nirmal Puraskar award instituted by the Government of India for Clean Village Campaign. Two months before the tsunami struck, Leepuram Panchayat was affected by a flood. Realizing the damage, the District Administration requested all Gram Panchayats to constitute a committee for "Disaster Management" as per the order passed by the Government of Tamil Nadu. No panahayat constituted the Disaster Management Committee except the Leepuram Panchayat. By realizing the importance of the Disaster Management Committee, he constituted a committee comprising women, Dalits, and representatives from all hamlets. The Village Development Committee Members and Ward Members were trained by a non-governmental organization, namely Covenet Centre for Development—through the District administration. This committee was formed on 19th August 2004. In Leepuram Panchayat, Arockiapuram hamlet was badly affected by the tsunami. Because of the committee's active participation people were saved.

Arockiapuram hamlet is an interior one in the Panchayat. So the non-governmental organizations, church representatives and the District Administration turned immediately towards that area because the Gram Panchayat President informed them about the tsunami to the District Collector, the parish priest and the Bishop over phone. They turned towards his Panchayat after his phone call and they assessed the damage with the help of the Panchayat President. The Panchayat took the responsibility and collected vital statistics and based on the basic information, damage was assessed by the officials. Without much controversy, a report was prepared for rehabilitation purposes. Simultaneously, a development plan was prepared for this Gram Panchayat. The Panchayat President evinced a keen interest and took the lead in all these activities. The President recommended to the District Administration and the parish priest to reconstruct the houses and to arrange for their livelihood. He also helped the Disaster Management Committee to reduce the damage. In all his activities he involved the committee members which in turn strengthened his hands.

Since the Panchayat President is so strong and vibrant, committed and got a name and recognition among the people and the officials, was able to manage the situation and carry out the activities effectively. He succeeded in all his attempts in this Gram Panchayat. The District Administration found that it was easy to work with this Gram Panchayat as it took responsibility. Of all the factors his honesty paid rich dividends in his activities.

Maintenance of Transparency Exhibiting Leadership Skills

Pushparajan, is currently Vice-President of Kovalam Panchayat. He was the Gram Panchayat President since 1989 till the enactment of the new Panchayat Raj System in Tamil Nadu. When the tsunami struck, two hamlets of Kovalam Panchayat, namely Kovalam and Siruvai Nagar were badly affected. After the first tsunami wave, he took the initiative and mobilized all youths and with the help of the youths and the parish priest, he rescued all the people and evacuated them to safer places. Even though the houses were very near the seashore, his immediate action saved all the people and there was no loss of life in this Panchayat. His action was timely and appreciated by everyone.

Later, with the help of the priest, the Gram Panchayat President conducted a workshop. All the affected people, scientists and the representatives of non-governmental organizations participated. With the help of the scientists, he initiated the construction of houses in safer places and the houses were disaster-proof. He contacted Loyola College, Chennai, and asked the college authorities to send volunteers for cleaning. The students came and cleaned the village with the help of the Gram Panchayat members. He is also a Nirmal Puraskar awardee. He arranged Rs. 10,000 for each physically challenged person after the tsunami and 45 persons were benefited by his intervention. He took the initiative for widow pension. All widows got this assistance. In this Panchayat, without waiting for instructions, he moved over to the reconstruction work. Moreover, he mobilised the people for activities which enabled the Panchayat carry out works very easily. Moreover, when he delivered the goods, people reposed greater confidence in him. In such a way he exhibited his leadership. The Panchayat leaders who were trained in disaster preparedness are sensitive towards gender issues.

Formation of Committees Representing All Communities, Distribution of Relief Through the Committees, Working Closely with Traditional Panchayat

V. Chandran, President of Kothattai Gram Panchayat of Parangipettai

Panchayat Union, Cuddalore District, has been praised by many as he expertly managed the crisis created by the tsunami in his Panchayat area. Basically a marine engineer (38) hailing from the fisher folk community, he was in the Middle East for some time to earn his livelihood. He returned to his village and contested in the Panchayat election and won. He carried out the Panchayat activities very effectively with the participation of all despite the opposition from some of his own community men especially after the election. It was purely an election feud. When he heard the news of the tsunami he was in a bus. Pudukkuppam was the worst affected area. The total death toll came to 126. Only six persons were in the village. Others had vacated the village after the tsunami hit that area. The six were involved in removing dead bodies. In fact, people living in other villages had the courage to visit the seashore and involved themselves in the rescue operation. Fishermen who lived in Pudupattinam who saw the tsunami waves refused to go to the village again. They experienced such a kind of trauma after witnessing the tsunami waves. The rescue team saved twelve persons. He went to the village and dead bodies were removed and identified. The Jammath came to the rescue of the villagers. They provided food and first aid to the affected families.

When all the dead bodies were brought to one place, the villagers refused to bury the dead bodies. Finally, the officials requested the Panchayat leaders to accept the dead bodies. People were in an agitating mood and refused to accept the dead bodies. They refused to burn or bury the dead bodies. Finally, he convinced the people. Since he took the responsibility to bring more number of people from outside to help the victims, people started believing him. Before the government started the rescue operation, the Panchayat President took the lead and, as a result, the government officials followed the President and he was supported by the government in attending to the needs of the people. The Panchayat President, with the help of the youth and the clerk, collected data. While doing this exercise, he consulted the traditional Panchayat leaders on every aspect of relief, rescue and rehabilitation. When he received relief material he openly maintained a notebook and the entire responsibility was given to the traditional Panchayat leaders. In fact, the traditional Panchayat leader was instrumental in opposing him in his Panchayat area right from the day of his election. When the data pertinent to the loss of life and property was consolidated, the Gram Sabha was asked to approve them. As such there was no dispute over the data as a *pucca* record system was maintained. He created an information centre in the

Panchayat office to disseminate information relating to the relief and rehabilitation works of the government and other donor agencies.

The Panchayat leader identified the location for a temporary shelter. Necessary facilities were provided at the temporary shelter by the Panchayat. Re-boring of a well was done by which good drinking water was supplied. Identity cards were prepared and issued to the affected 427 families. The Panchayat never allowed any agency to deal with the affected persons directly and, in the same way, the Panchayat never allowed the government officers to deal with the affected families directly. In all tsunami affected areas, data management became a big issue. In many of the Panchayats everyone was keeping a list of affected families and approached the donors and the government. But, in this Panchayat, there was only one list which was approved by the Gram Sabha and, endorsed by the traditional Panchayat leaders. He maintained a very good relationship with the traditional Panchayat leaders and he was always in consultation with the traditional Panchayat leaders.

Collection of material, storing of material and distribution of material for relief were done in a scientific way. He created a transparent system by which he distributed all the materials to the needy. He saw to it that no body other than the affected families got any relief material. His involvement in all the activities was from first day. He formed many committees for all activities in order to involve more number of people. Every activity was carried out through a committee. Even the Gram Sabha convened on 10th February 2005 to approve the beneficiaries' list, he allowed the people to examine each and every name included in the list. He invited the higher officials including the District Collector. He carried out activities in a transparent way.

He took special care of children and widows affected by the tsunami. Since the affected persons were getting huge sums from the government, their relatives showed keen interest in those individuals. To settle all the disputes in the best interests of the individuals, a lengthy dialogue was arranged with the involvement of the traditional Panchayat. Safety measures were taken to save the money given by the government to the affected persons, especially widows and children. All the money which the government gave was deposited in the banks.

He established a good rapport with the people and won their confidence which enabled him to have a firm contact with the government officials and NGO representatives. NGOs played a key role in clearing the entire village and now they are providing permanent shelters. He demonstrated his leadership by maintaining his cordiality with the traditional Panchayat leaders and all the other groups including his opponents who contested in the election. Further, he proved his transparent administration by constituting a committee for relief and distribution of relief material by incorporating a number of individuals from the traditional Panchayat leaders' group. On all occasions he went to the houses of others and never called anyone to his house. He was always responsive to the call of the public, NGOs and government officials. He took responsibility in managing the affairs. He was very firm and he maintained transparency in his dealings.

Box 20
Case of Aswini : A Tsunami Victim

Ms. Aswini, Tsunami victim got very good marks in 12th Standard. The President took her to the District Collector. With the District Collector's effort, she got admission in Kozhikode Medical College. Now she is pursuing her medical course in Kozhikode Medical College.

Obstacles Faced by the Panchayat

Many Panchayat Presidents faced obstacles and problems in establishing temporary shelters. The officials who were deputed to oversee the relief and rehabilitation did not listen to the words of the Panchayat Presidents.

In Prathabaramapuram Panchayat, the President requested the officials to establish temporary shelters in one place. But the officials did not listen and they constructed it in a different place and they used tin sheets. Within a few months after the tsunami, there was heavy rain. Rain water stagnated. It created a big problem. The tsunami occurred in the month of December. After three months, summer started. During summer tin sheets became very hot. Fishermen could not stay inside the house. Many suffered from heat related diseases. This created problems for the people and the Panchayat President.

Some people cut the fingers from the dead bodies and stole the gold rings and even they stole the *Mangal sutra* and gold chains off the dead bodies. People who lost their relatives suffered a lot; a lot of other people just wanted to collect freebies. The NGOs and the government distributed more relief material than required, e.g., one NGO distributed water packets. Immediately after half an hour another NGO distributed water bottles. So these people threw away the water packets and started collecting the water bottles.

In the beginning, affected people accepted old dresses. Once they started getting new one's, they started throwing the old ones away. The Panchayat President found it very difficult to clear the old dresses from many places; he did not know how to dispose of these old ones. Regarding the food packets each person got 10 to 12 food packets at a time. The next day everybody started throwing the remaining food packets. This also gave trouble to the Panchayat President to clear the food packets. In this regard, Prathabaramapuram Panchayat wasted nearly 10 tonnes of rice.

Many officials were biased towards the Panchayats. They concentrated only on fishermen because the officials misjudged that only the fishermen might have been affected; but, in fact, the non-fishermen like the land holders and Scheduled Castes were also affected. The lands of the farmers were damaged and the livestock possessed by the other families were also lost. Further, the houses of the non-fishermen community were also damaged; with regard to permanent shelters, the building is not strong by international standards. The ratio of cement and sand was not correct. Most of the houses are without toilets. The houses with toilets do not have septic tank in the Kameshwaram Panchayat.

In many places, there was conflict between the traditional and constitutional Panchayats. In Samiyarpettai Panchayat the constitutional Panchayat leader and self help group members underwent training in Disaster Management in the State Institute of Rural Development. When the tsunami occurred, a self help group member named Meera did excellent work during the tsunami. The Chief Minister appreciated her and honoured her by giving Rs. 5 lakhs. But the traditional Panchayat harassed her and they claimed that it was not an individual's work and it was group work. So, they argued that either she has to share with other Self Help Group members or with the traditional Panchayat. But she refused to share it either with SHGs or with traditional Panchayat. Also she migrated to somewhere else. Even on this small issue, the constitutional Panchayat was unable to solve the problem.

The government gave Rs. 30,000 to the damaged houses, but the traditional leaders shared this money with all the village people. So, it came down to Rs. 10,000 per family. In many Panchayats, there was no disaster management committee. The NGOs gave training only to SHGs in Disaster Management.

In Chinoor Pudhupettai of Cuddalore District, a big conflict arose within the traditional Panchayat and they were divided among themselves into three groups. The constitutional Panchayat was unable to keep them together at least for their children who lost their parents and got compensation of Rs. 50,000. But not all children who lost their parents got compensation. So, there was a conflict. The Panchayat President tried to solve the problem by writing letters to the officials. But the Panchayat did not have proper record on this matter. In the traditional Panchayat meetings, the leaders dominated and they did not allow women to speak in public and even they did not allow them to participate in the public meetings. But they allowed women to participate in self help group activities to get government benefits. Constitutional Panchayats could not sensitize the traditional Panchayat leaders on gender sensitivity.

In Kanyakumari District in some Panchayats, the parish priest worked in collaboration with the constitutional Panchayats where the President belonged to the same community and in some villages, they usually worked with the traditional Panchayats. Only with the consent of the parish priest, the government or any other organization could carry out relief and rehabilitation works in the Panchayats.

Another important problem faced by the Panchayats was in getting the exact figures about the affected and even the Panchayat was still struggling to get facts about the real losses. During the tsunami, officials were not sensitized on rehabilitation. As there was no relief code and disaster management policy in our state, it was utter confusion for several days.

Impact of Tsunami on the Coastal Community

"The tsunami created a concern of humanity in the community towards fellow beings", Manimaran told. There were a large number of relief and rescue activities which were in unexpected quantum. The fishermen had never thought that the world would come to their rescue at this magnitude. The compensation to the dead was really a consolation to the concerned family. But there were cases of wasteful expenditure by the family members, Manimaran observed. Due to the availability of money, the habitual drunkards spent lavishly on drinks, some others purchased motorbikes, and only poor families deposited their money in banks, Manimaran said. The tsunami had a lot of impact on the culture of the fishermen community. There are now occurrences of early marriage and the mindset of the youth has changed and they have come forward to marry girls with less dowry. After the tsunami, the youth desire a settled life, Manimaran felt.

Further, as the period of rehabilitation is a long one, the life style and willpower of the youth and adults among the fishermen has changed. Due to monthly doles, provision of household articles free of cost, free supply of rice and other necessary commodities to the affected families, a type of laziness has developed in the minds of the fishermen community. They have failed to muster courage to venture into the sea for fishing, Manimaran observed. Though the role of non-governmental organizations in relief and rescue activities was commendable, the standard of works they undertook was poor. Particularly, works like Food for Work Schemes were not carried out properly, Manimaran complained. Manimaran felt that there was confusion on the side of the government with regard to the drafting of permanent rehabilitation plans. Moreover, there was heavy damage for the farmers also. The agricultural land to an extent of one kilometre from the shore had been filled with sand and salt. The reclamation of these degraded lands has not yet been seriously taken up for discussion by the government, Manimaran felt. But, being a farmer as well as a fishermen, Manimaran is serious enough in providing all eligible assistance, both monetary and goods to all the families in the villages of Manickappangu Panchayat, whether they are farmers or fishermen or farm labourers.

Suggestions to Ensure a Larger Role for the Panchayats

Many Panchayats must have capacitated leaders with skill and efficiency and then they can manage any disaster. Government should form a Disaster Management Committee, consisting of the village administrative officer, block development officer, Tehsildar and other local officials; if any disaster occurs they must have proper coordination among themselves. The government must depend on the data finalized by the Gram Sabha on the loss of lives and properties for relief and compensation. Government must issue identity cards to all affected with the help of Panchayats; this should be ratified in the Gram Sabha. The Panchayat President must be consulted to identify the site for temporary and permanent shelters. Collection and distribution of relief materials should be done through Panchayats. Manimaran, the President of Manickappangu Panchayat, felt that the rescue and relief operations initiated by the government was not to the expected level. The survey and collection of data by the government officials were not seriously carried out. The relief packages did not properly reach the real victims. He also suggested that the construction of a tall tower-like building structure within 500 metres of the sea so that villagers can climb up and escape from the chasing waves.

In every coastal village, there should be a standing committee consisting of all stakeholders, i.e. representatives of government machinery, non-government institutions, traditional Panchayat committees and village Panchayat. They should meet periodically or whenever necessary and convey to the higher level authorities the experience of fishermen at sea during various seasons, the speed of wind, the magnitude of waves, the rainfall details, erosion of sand dunes, mangroves and other natural vegetation along the coastal area. This committee will not only be a disaster management committee but also a committee working for the protection and promotion of coastal-based socio-economic livelihood of all sections of the coastal area.

When a memorial was constructed in Poompukar for Kannaki, fishermen felt that it was only a protection wall for the memorial, but now they felt that because of the protected wall many people could save their lives. But everyone in the seashore area felt that a protection arrangement has to be made either by creating natural barriers or an artificial barrier. Over a period of time, the natural barriers have been removed by the people and government for their advantage. Now the time has come to create such a barrier by planting saplings of different varieties of trees as per the advice of the experts. In Chinoor Pudhupettai of Cuddalore District, the government decided to plant casuarinas to reduce damage from disasters like tsunami but they are not as good as mango trees. It has many drawbacks. They are:

(a) It is not a bush, it is a tree, so it will not reduce the force of the waves;
(b) Also public won't cut and use mango trees as they do with casuarinas;
(c) Mango trees add strength to the river bed, but not casuarinas;
(d) It is a benefit to government, because they are selling a plant for 50 paise;
(e) More than that, the mango plants will grow easily in salt water; and
(f) At least, the government has to plant the casuarinas. To meet any disaster, the Panchayat must have community-cum-relief hall with *pucca* construction. Further, there should be availability of vessels, utensils, and materials for the proposed construction.

The members of the fishermen community, though in fear of recurrence of tsunami like disaster, had a lesson and were getting ready to face the challenges, Manimaran explained. Manimaran suggested that the following arrangements to be provided in the coastal villages to handle the threat of tsunami:

(a) construction of a tall tower like building structure within 500 metres of the sea so that villagers can climb up and escape from the chasing waves;
(b) the construction should be sound enough to withstand the challenges like tsunami/heavy rain etc.;
(c) the habitation layout should be planned so as to have sufficient space between houses, broad streets, so that all can escape easily at the time of any threat;
(d) thorny bushes should be removed. Standing trees are not dangerous. On the contrary, they are saviors;
(e) there should be a big and spacious community centre with all infrastructure facilities. This should not be any type of temporary shelter; and
(f) guidance and further backward and forward linkages to those who are ready to have a new avocation other than fishing should be provided. As it is a customary practice in the fishermen families to engage anyone of their sons, if there are more than one son in the family, in fishing, it is possible to counsel these families to encourage the other young men to go to new avocations.

Life in the sea is always a struggle. It is always uncertain and yet they enjoy their life. They have witnessed several challenges in their life. Yet this tsunami has created an irremovable fear among the fishermen. Even if there is a small change in the height of the tide, they think of so many evils from the backdrop of the tsunami. The tsunami taught many lessons to the fishermen. Now one could find a change in the mindset and behaviour of the fishermen. When a memorial was constructed in Poompukar for Kannaki, fishermen felt that it was only a protection wall for the memorial. But now they felt that because of the protection wall many could save their lives. But everyone in the seashore area felt that a protection arrangement has to be made either by creating natural barriers or an artificial barrier. Over a period of time the natural barriers have been removed by the people and the government for their advantage.

Now the time has come to create such a barrier by planting saplings of different varieties of trees as per the advise of experts. People have witnessed that whenever natural barriers were created people had been saved as the velocity of the tide had been impeded. Now the community has realized the importance of natural barriers.

To meet any such disaster, Manimegalai proposed a system. A community-cum-relief hall with *pucca* construction is very much needed, she explained. Further, there should be availability of vessels, utensils, bedding and other livelihood facilities inside the proposed construction, she said. Based on Chandran's experience, he found that many gram Panchayat presidents exceptionally doing their duties. They need proper guidance and encouragement from the government, community and non-governmental organization. The district collector should meet the Panchayat president periodically. In one of the training camps conducted in RIRD, Arani, a retired teacher who became the gram Panchayat president gave a few suggestions. Each Gram Panchayat should prepare a vulnerability map. This vulnerability map should contain the following:

(a) Vulnerable persons in each family for example disabled persons and disabled children;
(b) Vulnerable families for example widows, women-headed families, families living in low lying areas; and
(c) The map should contain details about the access roads and escape roads. These access and escape roads should be marked in each village keeping sign boards in each road removing bushes and thorns from all roads. Fishermen's Panchayat, the villagers should attend the Gram Sabha.

As far as he concerned, if we are in one system, one should not criticize that system, we should try to maximize the profit from that system and reduce the bad things from that. The earlier government implemented a scheme called "Namadhu Gramam". It motivated the Gram Panchayat leaders to concentrate on "Social Development issues".

In Kothatai Panchayat, destitute women were living near water tank. He identified the problem of the destitute women, made them join the Self Help Group. He arranged vessels to start a refreshment stall from the Panchayat funds. Her name is Valli. Mr. Chandran does not live in the Panchayat area. He lives in Cuddalore for the sake of his children's study. If anyone needs his assistance at any time, he or she immediately calls him, within an hour, he reaches the Panchayat office. He never asks people to come and meet him. He makes sure that he goes to their area. He said proudly that in the 2006 Panchayat Elections, many contestants in the Cuddalore District cast their vote by quoting his achievements and saying that if they win, they will work like Mr. Chandran for the benefit of the people. As far as he was concerned, the Panchayat presidents should work for the people. His services were available to the needy people always. Even though people who do not know about the Panchayat win elections, they must learn about the Panchayat administration as quickly as possible.

Andhra Pradesh

Gram Panchayats have been created as per the confirmative legislation of the State Governments based on the spirit of the 73rd Constitutional Amendment to the Constitution of India.

1. Rural development and Panchayat Raj department are two different departments in Andhra Pradesh.
2. Election for the panchayat raj institutions are conducted by the panchayat raj department.
3. Jurisdictions for the Revenue Administration and the Development Administration are the same.
4. The Mandal level officials from the Department of Education, Health, Agriculture and Animal Husbandry should have linkages with the Panchayati Raj Institution.
5. Mandal Level Development Officer and Mandal Revenue Officer should sit with the District Collector in the video conferencing. They should discuss flood and disaster management plans apart from the implementation of the development schemes.
6. Secretaries should be appointed in the Junior Assistant scale for the village panchayats.

Roles and Responsibilities

Panchayats must perform the following functions:

(a) Taking care of Sanitation,
(b) Lighting, Street lights,
(c) Prevention of communicable diseases,

(d) Creating drinking water facilities,
(e) Renovation of the roads and buildings that are in the area of the Panchayat,
(f) Digging drainages for allowing the seepage of water and rain water from the villages,
(g) Making arrangements for keeping the streets clean, removing bushes, thorny plants, and other useless weeds and trees from the villages, filling the damaged wells, low lands, useless ponds and ditches. Maintaining the sanitation of the Panchayat,
(h) Construction of public latrines, personal latrines and maintaining them,
(i) Allocating burial ground and maintaining them for cremating dead bodies and dead animals also,
(j) Preventing contagious diseases from spreading and treating the existing patients,
(k) Creating water resources for drinking, bathing and for washing clothes by digging wells or ponds or constructing tanks, their maintenance and repairing are also the duties of the Panchayats,
(l) Making arrangements for compost preparation, protecting manure resources and selling manure,
(m) Birth and death registration is the most important duty of the Panchayat,
(n) Registering marriages,
(o) Preparing micro level local plans for maintaining the natural resources,
(p) Maintenance of cattle ponds,
(q) Establishing libraries, reading rooms and their maintenance,
(r) Taking up rehabilitating activities for disabled, destitute and chronic patients,
(s) Maintaining nurseries, producing and supplying better varieties of seeds,
(t) Organizing exhibitions for propagating better methods of farming,
(u) Establishing helping centres during calamities and natural disasters, and
(v) Encouraging cottage industries and micro-level business enterprisers.

In Andhra Pradesh, all hamlets have telephone facilities. The village level officers inform the public about flood warning through usual methods such as "Tom-Tom". At the Mandal level, the MROs should have wireless sets.

In each district, the Revenue department should prepare an action plan under the supervision of the district collector in the month of May and September each year. This plan should contain a list of vulnerable villages and cyclone mitigation meetings should be organized at the district and mandal level. The tahsildar should act as the coordinator at the mandal level meetings. The Special Officers will be appointed at the gram Panchayat level. Services of the government teachers will be utilized during the monsoon season. Pucca relief centres will be there in all the necessary locations. Otherwise, school buildings will be converted as relief centres. Based on the ration card (White ration card), essential commodities will be distributed. Rice will be stocked at fair price shops. Relief teams will undertake relief operations. The enumeration officer will prepare the damage list like house damages, cattle loss, tank breaches etc. The medical team will keep medicines ready, after preparing the list of the beneficiaries, relief measures will be taken after the due approval from the District Collector. This will be taken as per the government orders.

Kottapattinam Panchayat, Govindapillai SC Colony, Kota Mandal

There are nine villages in Kottapattinam Panchayat, all social categories of the people BC, SC, ST and OC are in this Panchayat. Cyclone and floods are regular phenomenon. The disasters have affected the panchayat in the following years:

(a) 1984: Cyclone; (b) 2001, 2004, 2005, 2006: Floods; (c) 2004: Cyclone.

If Buckhimgham canal desilted properly, flood water could recede through it. Apart from this, tanks and other canals are there in this panchayat. Flood and cyclone warning is given by the MRO. He passes the information over a phone to village revenue officers. The Government of Andhra Pradesh does not form disaster management committees at the village/Panchayat level.

Thirupalaiah, President of Kottapattinam Panchayat, feels that disaster management committees should be formed in each village and people must be trained. Community must be sensitized to take ownership of the committee. The panchayat can perform the coordinating role. In this Panchayat, the NGOs have formed a number of committees, they are, (a) protection committee, (b) first aid committee, (c) food security committee, (d) rescue committee (members are only male), (e) shelter committee.

Each committee comprises three men and two women except the rescue committee. During floods and cyclone, the NGOs distribute rice and *dal*. The Group members take loan from their savings. Apart from that, the NGO provides (a) seedlings, (b) assistance for petty shops, (c) fish vending, (d) goats, and (e) fish nets.

In the ST colony, there are 30 houses, but there is no electricity. The government of Andhra Pradesh has implemented many schemes such as Indramma Model Panchayat. Through this, all-around development activities are taken up. The Speak India has established village sustainable development committees. In that, the Sarpanch is the President and the village elders are called "Kappu". If the Sarpanch is active, he concentrates on the problems related to ration shop, *anganwadi* etc.

Box 21
Case of Katari Nagamma

Katari Nagamma, 38 year old illiterate woman was elected to the office of the president of Baduhuvani Lanka Panchayat. She belongs to the SC community and she has eleven children. This Panchayat is Kappu dominated. There were six contestants in the recent Gram Panchayat election. The high caste elected Katari Nagamma as the president. In the beginning she could not work independently after attending EWRs network meeting, she slowly realized her strength and started to work independently. Her achievement is that she has mobilized all women in the Panchayat. Everyday each women put one hand full of rice in the Panchayat storing place. After six months, they sell the rice and deposit the amount in the SHG's account. If heavy flood comes they use that rice. She also works for the betterment of women.

In the Adivasi Dalit association

1. There is no unity among them,
2. Frequent change of leadership,
3. Lack of gender equity, and
4. No proper planning.

Present Status of the Panchayati Raj Institutions in Andhra Pradesh

Both Telugu Desam and the Congress always keep low profile on the PRIs. The Panchayati Raj Institutions can prepare contingency plans based on them, the government should allocate resources for disaster management. But the local body institutions have not yet initiated this process. People have to be educated on local body institutions. They have to demand and claim their entitlements. The secretary of the gram Panchayats are dominating and overshadowing the elected body. The panchayat has to be given powers to appoint the secretaries. There are always rifts between secretaries and the Presidents. The local bodies should be strengthened in an institutional perspective. In a few places, the local bodies are working well and they doing so due to various reasons. The Fisheries Department has rights to auction the Panchayat tanks. In many places before the entry of the Fisheries Department, Panchayats had auctioned and owned the tanks.

It has been noted that the Panchayat leaders' socio-economic background is an important factor for the success of the panchayats. The Sarpanch should not be compelled to do the disaster management and mitigation activities. Wherever the NGOs had intervened, a large number of people have participated in the Gram Sabha meetings. Prior to the NGOs' intervention, only the Sarpanch and the panch conducted the Gram Sabha and passed resolutions and send them to the government. The NGOs' intervention motivated the people. They realized about their rights and the importance of Gram Sabha and started attending Gram Sabha. A few NGOs have conducted training programmes to the elected representatives on their rights and it strengthens the local body institutions. The upper caste and traditional leaders dominate the elected representatives. The tribal people do not have land rights. The traditional leaders have captured the tribal lands and made tribal leaders landless. Nobody sells the lands or buy it. The NGO urged the Andhra Pradesh Government to implement PESA Act.

The Village Panchayats have Vidya Vikas Committees. The study found that there is a weak leadership in the Panchayati Raj Institutions. The Gram Panchayat mainly concentrates on implementing the Government schemes like National Rural Employment Scheme, Indramma Aadarsha Gramam, Pasu Kranthi, MLA and MP schemes. Under MLA and MP schemes the building of houses and schools are under progress. The study found that there is no active role of the NGOs for strengthening the Local Governance. The road connectivity is very poor to the hamlets. In Rural areas access to higher education is limited. Child labour practices prevail in many places. The SHGs get loans at the lowest interest. With the loans, the SHG women are taking a number of activities. Staff strength is very poor in the panchayats. A single clerk works for three or four panchayats. Extension officers of the panchayats are the main officers at the mandal level. But due to the large number of panchayats in each mandals, the officers are unable to give proper guidance and supervise the panchayat activities. The Government is concentrating more on its implementing schemes, rather than establishing governance system at the Grassroots level. But preparation of BPL list is done in a participatory way and sectoral level officials are participating in the preparation of the BPL list. Pension schemes are implemented through the panchayats. The Panchayat leaders don't have a vision for the development and there is no strong women leadership.

Gujarat

In accordance with the 73rd Constitutional Amendment Act the Government of Gujarat enacted the Gujarat Panchayat Raj Act and it has a three-tier structure. Gram Panchayat (Jute Panchayat), Block Panchayat and District Panchayat. The following roles and responsibilities have been given to the Gram Panchayats:

1. Providing basic amenities like water, sanitation, health.
2. Maintaining *anganwadis* and check dams.

The Government of Gujarat have appointed clerks for every panchayat in the cadre of Junior assistants but they function from the Block Headquarters. In Gujarat, after the first earthquake, the Gram Panchayat elections had been postponed by an ordinance in the month of December 2000, as the state was facing severe drought. At the time of the earthquake (January 26, 2001), the administration of the gram Panchayats were under the administrators. However, the Taluk and District Panchayat elections had been conducted before the earthquake. The earthquake rehabilitation package announced by the Government spelt out that to avoid top-down approach, the Instrumentality of the Gram Sabha was approved. According to the UNFPA and Unnati, it has been observed that the PRIs were the first to respond to organize relief and rescue work, however, in providing long-term rehabilitation, the PRIs capacity and credibility have been questioned. There are two major problems in involving the Panchayats in relief and rehabilitation activities. (i) Lack of faith in the Panchayats, and (ii) low credibility of the Panchayats, and the question of their capacity. The Government of Gujarat has a unique scheme called Samaras. In that if any panchayat selects president and its ward members unanimously, that panchayat will get Rs. 1 lakh from the Government as an incentive.

For the purpose of disaster management, an authority was established which gives recommendations to the district. The District Collector is expected to:

(a) Assist the authority, the commissioner;
(b) Ensure that the staff of the local authority is trained;
(c) Ensure that the resources related to disaster management are so maintained as to be ready for use;
(d) Ensure that all buildings and other structures in the local area comply with the specification laid down in this behalf by the departments of government and the authority;
(e) Carry out relief operations in the affected area subject to the directions of the Commissioner;
(f) Carry out reconstruction and rehabilitation activities in accordance with the guidelines framed by the authority;
(g) Prepare a disaster management plan setting out the following, namely,
    (i) the manner in which the concept and principles of disaster management are to be applied in the local area;
    (ii) role and responsibilities of the local authority in the terms of the disaster management plan of the state;
    (iii) capacity of the local authority to fulfil its role and responsibility;
    (iv) particulars of disaster management strategies;
    (v) contingency strategies and emergency procedures in the event of a disaster, including measures to finance the strategies;
(h) Coordinating the preparation and the implantation of plans with those of the organizations of the state and stakeholders;
(i) Regularly review and update the plans;
(j) Conduct disaster management drills periodically; and
(k) Provide such assistance to the authority, the Commissioner and the Collector to take such other steps as may be necessary for disaster management.

Each local authority shall submit to the authority and the commissioner a copy of its disaster management plan proposed under sub-section (1) and any amendment thereto. Few NGOs giving Capacity building for strengthening Panchayats in grassroots levels.

As per the Gujarat Panchayat Act, the Panchayat has to work for the following activities with regard to disasters. All relief materials should be distributed through Panchayats. Whenever government implement schemes through NGOs in particular Panchayats. Panchayats have freedom to select NGOs. Gram Panchayat has to get approval from the Gram Sabha.

Box 22
GSDMA Efforts

According to GSDMA officials, the January 26, 2001, the earthquake in Gujarat cost widespread damage and destruction over 13,805 lives were lost, 1,67,000 were injured and over a million houses were destroyed or severely damaged. There was a large scale damage to vital social and physical infrastructure. Government undertook massive rehabilitation and reconstruction work with the help of NGOs and community, a district level advisory committee was formed in that district panchayat, president is one of the members. The village level reconstructive committee consists of Sarpanch, Ex-Sarpanch, women member of the Panchayat, representatives from SC/ST and Minority community.

Traditional structures are strong in Gujarat. The traditional leaders and community representatives selecting most of the Panchayat presidents and they are deciding all Panchayat activities. Government of Gujarat is also encouraging traditional leaders to occupy the Panchayat and women participation in Panchayats are very weak.

One of the village named Timba in Vaduvan Block of Surendranagar District was affected by various disasters such as drought in 1988 had a severe impact and 2002-03 drought for few months, Earthquake in 2001, and flood in 2005. It was informed by Ganga Das Bai (President) of the village that "when we face any disaster in the village both constitutional and traditional Panchayats work together. Though we have different views on various issues, we work together when it comes to village development. He said that eight years back there was a fire incident in a cotton store. There was no water source in that store and hence people had been asked to help. The entire community put mud on fire and put down the fire. There the leaders realized the power of the people when they are united. After this incidence communities from both traditional Panchayat and constitutional Panchayat came together and constructed, a pond. And also with the intervention of AIDMI (NGO) who started giving awareness towards various disasters, community were able to cope up with various losses in future. In Timba village, Vadvam Block, Surendranager District of Gujarat, one of the traditional leaders acted as a bridge between the village Panchayat president and all India Disaster Management Institute (AIDMI), Ahmedabad. Since last three years, due to heavy flood, village farmers faced huge loss. Since the traditional leaders having a good relation with AIDMI, conducted water audit with the community and found that there is enough water but no proper storage facilities as a solution to have a check dam, which may protect the crops to some extent from floods. To build the check dam, the traditional leaders gave some piece of land and also helped to get lands from the community. For constructing the check dam, the AIDMI planned to give 75 per cent of funds and the community contributed 25 per cent and the community also extended the labour support in the construction process. This check dam is now safeguarded the farmers from flood during winter. In this village, the communities say only men will act as traditional leaders and every year they select one traditional leader from each community or regionwise. In Gujarat, the traditional leaders from the dominating caste dominate the Panchayat.

The study found that Panchayat representatives involved themselves in relief, rehabilitation work till the entry of outsiders, distribution of relief materials through committees but, during the rehabilitation work, government, national and international donor agencies bypassed the Panchayats. The panchayat leaders lack the information about government packages. This made them very miserable, they could not answer the people's queries.

PART II : INTERFACE BETWEEN TRADITIONAL PANCHAYATS AND CONSTITUTIONAL PANCHAYATS

Orissa

In each village the persons from the wealthiest family are considered as traditional leaders. Communities depend on them for conducting temple festivals to sorting out minor conflicts. But they do not involve in developmental activities and panchayat activities. They haven't involved in Disaster Management Activities. Relief, Rehabilitation and Reconstruction activities are carried out through DMT, Panchayats or SHGs.

Tamil Nadu

After the tsunami struck, the local people who first rushed and carried out all evacuation work right from saving drowning people to recovering bodies, providing food and shelter. During the rescue operations, it was very hard to walk freely. There were thorns and broken logs which struck against feet and fingers. It was tough. Ordinary persons could not withstand such a struggle, Manimaran said. Only able bodied individuals could engage in relief work like tsunami relief, he said. When they all were engaged in identifying dead bodies, they found one woman trapped between a gate and a wall and the wall fell on her and squeezed her to death. To remove the body, the cement gate had to be lifted up. But it was not easy to do so due to its weight. Manimaran and some youths jointly made an attempt and they were able to remove the dead body. Manimaran felt that it was a horrible scene to recollect. Manimaran shared that the rescue and relief operations initiated by the government were not to the expected level. The survey and collection of data by the government officials were not seriously carried out. The relief packages were not properly reached to the real sufferers, he complained. In most of the fishing villages, the presence of strong traditional structure or fish workers federation wanted the relief work routed only through them. They prepared the list of affected people and the damaged properties. Even though this traditional community played important role in keeping the morale of the community and bringing affected people together, they lacked the following:

(a) Lack of sensitivity on equity concept;
(b) Lack of gender sensitivity;
(c) Not considering women-headed households;
(d) Not considering the dalits and other communities; and
(e) They are not sensitive about orphans and physically challenged people.

Pudukuppam, the affected hamlet of Kothatai Panchayat was chosen for the construction of 87 houses. But there was no poramboke land to construct 87 houses in one place. If they construct houses in some other place instead of Pudukuppam, they thought that the bonding among themselves will weaken, and they become indifferent to the Panchayat people. The traditional panchayat members consulted Mr. Chandran. As per Mr. Chandran's advice, the traditional panchayat decided to purchase land to construct houses at one place. As per the government order, the government could pay only Rs. 30,000 per acre to construct houses for Tsunami Victims. But in Pudukuppam Panchayat, land value of one acre was Rs. 1,00,000.

The Committee consisting of Mr. Chandran discussed the issues and devised a plan. As per their plan, land could be purchased at the cost of Rs. 1,00,000 per acre. The remaining amount apart from government's construction funds could be collected from the beneficiaries and paid to the land sellers. As per their plan, 4 acres of land was purchased at the cost of Rs. 4 lakh. The government paid Rs. 1,20,000. Remaining Rs. 2,80,000 was collected from the beneficiaries. Each beneficiary paid Rs. 2700 and it came around to Rs. 2,34,900. Mr. Chandran sold his own 2 acres of land for constructing Tsunami victims' houses. The committee of traditional leaders decided that, 85 houses should be allotted for Tsunami victims, one house for the person who helped a lot during the time of Tsunami and one house for Chandran's parents. All beneficiaries accepted the committee's recommendations and put their signatures.

In the meantime, 2 Tsunami victims met the press and complained about Chandran that he got Rs. 2700 from each beneficiary to allot the houses. It became an issue Mr. Chandran got depressed, because he took all steps with the consultation of the community but still, a few in the community blamed him. He put his resignation papers to the District Collector Mr. Gagandeep Singh Bedi. Mr. Bedi had faith on Mr. Chandran, and refused to accept his resignation. He sent Mr. Arun Roy, the Sub-Collector for an enquiry.

Mr. Arun Roy, the Sub-Collector came to Pudukuppam with the Tehsildar, Revenue officials and police. He convened the Gram Sabha to look into the matter. He started his enquiry. He called persons who lodged the complaint to the media. They said that they never agreed with the committee's decisions and they never put their signature. He asked them to put their signatures in front of all. They again put their signatures. He found that both the signatures were the same and he found out the truth. He warned, the few (who took up the matter to the media) that if they create problem like this, he will get a complaint from the Panchayat president and put them in jail. Again the District Collector called him Mr. Chandran and advised him that people who are working for the people should not be emotional.

Andhra Pradesh

Traditional structures are very strong and they are called Kappu and they decide the activities in a particular village. In many of the places, they block the development activities. The chief of the NGO, Speak India said that the traditional leaders are not gender sensitized, they are harassing women. If anyone talks against them, he or she is intimidated. The Scheduled Castes and Scheduled Tribes work in the fields of the landlords and the traditional leaders. Their livelihood depend on them. With respect to disaster management, the traditional structures decide about the relief activities.

Gujarat

Traditional structures are strong in Gujarat. The traditional leaders and community representatives selecting most of the Panchayat presidents and they are deciding the all Panchayat activities. Government of Gujarat also encouraging traditional leaders to occupy the Panchayat and women participation in Panchayats are very nominal.

One of the villages named Timba in Vaduvan Block of Surendranagar District was affected by various disasters such as drought in 1988 and had a severe impact and in 2002-2003 drought for a few months, the earthquake in 2001, and flood in 2005. It was informed by Ganga Das Bai (President) of the village that "when we face any disaster in the village both constitutional and traditional Panchayats work together. Though we have different views on various issues, we work together when it comes to the village development". He said that eight years back there was a fire incident in a cotton store. There was no water source in that store and hence people were asked to help. The entire community put mud on the fire and put down the fire. There the leaders realized the powers of the people when they are united. After this incident, the communities from both traditional Panchayat and constitutional Panchayat came together and dug a pond. And also with the intervention of AIDMA (NGO) who started giving awareness of the various disasters, the people were able to cope up with various losses. In Timba village, Vadvam Block, Surendranager District of Gujarat, one of the traditional leaders acted as a bridge between the village Panchayat president and the All India Disaster Mitigation Institute (AIDMI), Ahemedabad. In the last three years, due to heavy flood, village farmers faced huge losses.

Since the traditional leaders having a good relation with AIDMI, took up water audit with the community and found that there was enough water but no proper storage facilities, so a solution to construct a check dam, which might protect the crops to some extent from the floods. To build the check dam three traditional leaders gave some piece of land and also helped to get lands from the community. For constructing the check dam, the AIDMI planned to give 75 per cent of funds and the community contributed 25 per cent and the community also extended the labour support in the construction process. This check dam now safeguards the farmers from flood during winter. In this village, the communities say only men will act as traditional leaders and every year they will select one traditional leader from each community or regionwise. So, there are more number of traditional leaders in the villages. In Gujarat, the traditional leaders from the dominating caste dominate the Panchayat too.

To sum up, panchayats have the capability to carry out disaster preparedness and disaster management. In Tamil Nadu, many panchayat leaders had exhibited their capacity during tsunami disaster. In Andhra Pradesh, a few leaders had the capacity to carry out the relief activities. They were regularly attending the district level meetings. In Gujarat, a few NGOs trained the panchayat leaders on disaster management. Now they take up rehabilitation activities. In Orissa, panchayats are part of the Cyclone Shelter Management Committee, DMT. House benefits should be distributed through panchayat. If there is hunger in any Panchayat, it is the responsibility of the panchayat to provide food. Need of the hour is to strengthen panchayats in the disaster management aspects. It should be part of their regular activities along with development activities. Trained, sensitized leaders will manage disasters effectively. So leadership matters.

6

Findings, Recommendations and Suggestions

There are numerous important lessons to be learnt from the ways relief, rehabilitation and reconstruction efforts have been undertaken. In the tsunami regions there are a few pertinent lessons to be learnt from disaster mitigation and preparedness. We have discussed many issues in the previous chapters. Based on the study the following are the major findings:

Orissa

- Before the 1999 super cyclone, no significant role was played by the local community and panchayati raj institutions in Disaster Management. After 1999 cyclone INGOs gave training to the communities and panchayati raj representatives. They concentrated more towards preparedness. Distribution of relief materials to the affected and activities carried out through panchayati raj institutions made the delivery system more efficient and transparent resulting in greater satisfaction amongst the flood-affected people. However, it appeared that the members of the panchayat raj institutions and the community were not taken into confidence while drawing up plans for restoration, reconstruction and rehabilitation by the officials. House building assistance was given through village panchayats. The Government of Orissa is planning to construct 6000 godowns in gram Panchayats. This kind of structures have strengthened the Panchayats.
- In 2001, the Orissa flood damage assessment was done by the revenue officials. No role was given to gram panchayats. While damages to the public property was taken care of by the respective departments promptly, house damage, crop and land loss assessments were undertaken quite late (according to the

perception of the committee). There were practical difficulties in assessing damages to the houses and sand accumulation on cultivable lands. The time lag in damage assessment adversely affected the rehabilitation plans in many cases.

- NGOs formed women groups and trained them in the disaster preparedness. UNDP played a major role in initiating community-based disaster management programme. Red Cross trained the volunteers actively participating in rescue operations during disaster. Orissa State Disaster Management Authority was formed and actively functioned in this process of preparedness. Early Warning System—ICT centres were being established by NGOs with the help of government but they are not very active. Mass media like radio is properly utilized for dissemination of information regarding flood warning and people are trained to respond immediately after the early warning system. Traditional Panchayats are oriented more in conventional activities than in developmental activities. They are not participating in panchayat activities. Village Panchayat committees looked after relief works. But few NGOs distributed relief materials through SHGs.
- Hamlet-wise committees were constituted. There was no integration between these committees and village Panchayats. Relief activities were carried out through village Panchayats in more efficient way. There was no proper linkages among the committees of blocks and districts. Disaster preparedness activities were initiated by OSDMA with the help of INGOs, NGOs and UNDP. NGOs prepared the community by involving women. 30 per cent of the women representatives were involved in all committees. Network between NGO and government were strengthened through OSDMA. Food and essential commodities were stored in village godown by NGOs. Organising of women was the main focus of the NGO. Coordination among communities was more. Volunteers are trained as ToT. These trained volunteers in turn train villagers on disaster preparedness.
- Relief code emphasize Disaster Management Policy and PRIs role is clearly stated in relief code and disaster management policy. Preparation and execution of relief work should be with the involvement of panchayats. Accountability of officer in-charge of the relief circle ensured the association of peoples' representative. The Chairman of Panchayat Samiti is invited to

attend the committee meetings. During famine, the panchayat has to provide food to starving people for example if a starved person from a nearby panchayat needs food he must be provided with food without getting any permission from BDOs.

- Undertaking labour intensive work in the Panchayats is carried out and they are authorized to make labour budgeting. Arrangement of food material and stocking of food grains in the office of the Panchayat was an expected work. Provision of drinking water was the main duty of the Panchayat. The relief code is yet to become a reality now. The NGOs are exerting pressure on the government to legalize the code. In respect of maintaining downward accountability—there is a lack of sensitization among the stakeholders towards social accountability. A proper system to uphold downward accountability is absent.
- The potential of Gram Sabha is not yet realized. The impact of 1999 Super Cyclone is realized and government is giving much attention to preparedness creating early warning system. Empowering the community is also realized and training is given to community members, especially, women and volunteers.

Tamil Nadu

- Even before the occurrence of tsunami, Government of Tamil Nadu issued an order to form disaster preparedness committees in each Panchayat. A few Panchayat leaders formed committees with a sense of commitment. In general, all Panchayats just listed some members even without their knowledge. A few Panchayat Presidents received training in disaster preparedness by the initiative of UNDP and Government of Tamil Nadu. The trained Gram Panchayat presidents were helpful to evacuate the needs of the affected people and put them in the nearby panchayat. Prior training helped them to realize the importance of taking the following measures: They took efforts to inject TT as precaution. They mobilized youngsters and assembled them in one place. They acted immediately in this regard. Photographs of the dead bodies were taken by the Gram Panchayat presidents and informed District Collectors so that the dead bodies in bad condition could be buried without any post mortem. Sensitized Panchayat

Presidents immediately responded towards tsunami involved themselves with traditional community till the entry of outsiders. Lack of gender sensitivity among traditional Panchayat leaders made women miserable even though NGOs and INGOs had gender policy and they had been working closely with traditional Panchayat structures. Women headed households did not get relief materials in many Panchayats.

- The vulnerable sections did not get any recognition. No specific care and attention was given to vulnerable people during the relief and rehabilitation. UNDP and Government of Tamil Nadu installed Early Warning System after tsunami in Cuddalore district but did not cover the entire coastal area. The location of EWS is not proper and not easily accessible. In respect of entrusting responsibility in handling of the system was not properly delegated.

Information Communication Technology Centres were established by NGOs and INGOs. But there was no proper coordination among them as well as with other stakeholders for example in P.R. Puram Panchayat, three NGOs established ICT centres. Most of the time, these ICT centres remained closed and they did not share the information among themselves and with community but the Hunger Project established agriculture information centre in Kameshwaram panchayat and they appointed a retired officer from the agriculture department in the same area. He was regularly interacting with the community and shared the information about the agricultural activities.

- There was lack of adequate training in respect of utilizing the EWS and other technology to the stakeholders in many Panchayats in Cuddalore district. The EWS did not merge with the existing Panchayat system. So in many Panchayats, the leaders were not owning responsibility on EWS. Domination of traditional Panchayat leaders is obvious in many of the villages except in a few, where constitutional Panchayat leaders are trained and they took a lead after tsunami struck.
- Lack of democracy in the functioning of traditional Panchayat is obvious. There is no women in Traditional Panchayat Council. In many Panchayats the traditional Panchayats kept changing the leadership just to attract more money from the INGOs. Within a

month after tsunami struck, the traditional Panchayat leaders came to know about INGOs and they started demanding more funds. There was no systematic interface between traditional panchayats and constitutional panchayats due to the domination of traditional panchayat leaders. NGOs directly dealt with the traditional Panchayats in spite of the lack of faith in equity and gender insensitivity. There was no proper sensitization among the officials, NGOs and INGOs on Panchayati Raj Institutions. Several Panchayat Presidents did not realize their role and responsibilities in disaster management.

- Sensitized Panchayat Presidents joined together with the traditional Panchayats and successfully carried out relief and rehabilitation activities. They ensured the coordination among the government functionaries and departments, and sensitized the Village Panchayat Presidents and responded quickly by establishing contacts with the affected persons, and helped them to move to safe places.

They made initial arrangements for the affected people food, drinking water, clothing and other basic needs. According to the president of Kameshwaram Panchayat, the Panchayat area is sandy so the sand suck the water quickly hence the village was affected by the flood miserably: the structure of the village is that it is surrounded by sand dunes and trees on both the sides. Only one side is low laying area, so the sand dunes and trees safeguarded the people from the sea water. Further, if at all the sea water entered the village, the water rushed out to the low lying area so the water did not stagnate in that village. The deaths occurred not only due to sea water, but also because of the trees that fell on the people.

During the cyclone and heavy rainy seasons—the thatched houses because of their light weight which did not fall down easily. So loss of life was meagre; but, the tiles made up of mud got moistened and broke into pieces and fell. Each piece was like a stone and caused more injuries. To be safe from earthquake, some village people in Gujarat, preferred to have the traditional type of houses made up of light roof materials and thin round shape walls pasted with cowdung and cameldung.

The study found that the training to the Gram Panchayat President is important, in relief and rehabilitation activities. Relief activities started by the government only after three days of the occurrence. The food packets provided by the government were not eatable. Instead of providing food packets, government could have made arrangements to prepare food on the spot with the help of community and Panchayats.

- Linkages with block and district committees have not yet been initiated.
- The process of building up of disaster preparedness among the local body institutions has been initiated by the Government of Tamil Nadu and UNDP. Generally NGOs are not yet coming forward in building up disaster preparedness. They concentrated more on relief instead of involving community and empowering them. It has been noticed that there is no culture of working together and through a system. The role of women and Dalits in relief and rehabilitation activities did not get attention of the relief agencies. They were side-lined and due representation was not given to them. The impact of tsunami on Dalit habitation and livelihood was not immediately realized. In respect of relief and rehabilitation activities there was no relief code and management policy from the perspective of grassroots institutions.
- Traditional knowledge, wisdom and practices are not given recognition which resulted in wastages of resources, duplication and delay in the execution of relief and rehabilitation activities. All activities were supply-driven not on demand-driven. Even after the bitter experiences, lessons were not learnt from the past. In the 1977 Vedaranyam Flood, the Government forecast made the people stay inside the houses. This reduced human loss.
- Committees which were constituted did not work properly. No training was given to the committee members. Plans for preparedness has not yet been drafted in Tamil Nadu.

Andhra Pradesh

Many districts of Andhra Pradesh are suffering from seasonal floods, cyclone and drought. Flood in the river Godavari is a regular phenomena. The government of Andhra Pradesh formed district level flood management committees headed by the District Collector and it is functioning effectively. The state level officials have contacts with district collectors through video conferences. In the video conferences apart from the District Collector, Mandal Revenue Officer and Mandal Developmental Officer participated.

The Government of Andhra Pradesh involves village-wise representatives, teachers, field staff of the government departments in the flood management work. Once the warning is given, they are requested to move to the assigned villages to do precautionary measures and relief activities.

No specific role was assigned to PRIs but they are the members of the district level committees, most of the leaders do not participate in district level meetings called by the District Collector due to lack of awareness. The flood management communities were formed and sensitized by the NGOs. The committee comprises community representatives. These communities responded well during flood situations. Community flood management fund was mobilized by the NGOs. Officials did not have gender sensitivity in carrying out the activities. The self help groups were not properly oriented in disaster preparedness. They mostly concentrate on savings and credit. Early Warning System has been established in a well coordinated manner by the Government of Andhra Pradesh. Seasonal disaster impact were properly assessed by the government of Andhra Pradesh flood level had been monitored by the revenue officials and they were regularly disseminate the information regarding natural disasters to the community.

Necessary activities for preparedness were initiated by the district level committee. With regard to flood and disaster management, adequate powers were granted to the revenue officials by the government of Andhra Pradesh. Attitude of the revenue officials and community decided the role of PRIs in village level flood management committees and other relief and rehabilitation activities. Traditional structures are very strong one. They even sometimes work against the development initiatives.

Minimum role has been assigned to the constitutional panchayats due to establishment of various parallel bodies in gram Panchayats. No specific role was assigned to gram Panchayats with regard to disaster management. District and mandal committees have been dominated by the officials. There is a lack of awareness about the committees and their functioning among the Presidents of gram Panchayats and the people in the village. Organising of women is the main activity of the NGOs. Representation has been given to each caste member in the hamlet committees to manage disaster. One could find coordination among the communities. Volunteers are trained as master trainers. There is no specific relief code. But, Godavari's Manual on Flood Management of the Godavari river is available which focuses on the formation of committees, activities of preparedness and systems of coordination.

With regard to Disaster Management Committees, the Government of Andhra Pradesh has Mandal level disaster teams in which the MRO, Panchayat leaders of that Mandal, Teachers, PRO and individuals from each village are members. Every year they meet twice in the months of May and September and plan to protect the people from floods. The villages of Nellore district have two teams, namely, Relief Team and Medical Team. The Panchayats store necessary rice and groceries. During disasters, the village relief team collects the details regarding the affected families and places them before MRO and the same is passed on to the District Collector and after his approval the relief materials are provided. But, Many Panchayat leaders do not attend these meetings due to lack of awareness about this committee, so many Panchayats do not avail the services of the government.

In Andhra Pradesh, few NGOs collaborate with Panchayats in all disaster management activities but in general the Panchayat Raj Institutions of Andhra Pradesh are functioning according to the guidance of the government and the organizations working in the village. Many Panchayat bodies do not know about their own role in disaster management and about the roles and responsibilities in disaster management. But, those leaders who are cooperate with the government and the organizations succeed in getting all facilities to the Panchayat. Primarily, the relief activities in every Panchayat are undertaken only by the organizations working in the villages. Before the organization's entry the people used to suffer till the government entered, and such a situation exists in many villages even now.

Gujarat

Major impact of an earthquake made the Gujarat government to form village level committees. In the village level committees the representation was given to all communities. The representatives were selected from each community and they formed disaster management committees. Panchayats are entrusted with the responsibilities of coordinating of government departments with communities during disaster management. Distribution of relief materials was carried out through out the village level committees by involving Panchayats. Food grains were distributed instead of ready-made food. Gujarat State Disaster Management Authority had been constituted. It has designed 30 types of model houses. People had opportunity to choose. The level of damage of the houses was assessed by NGO and Government with the participation of communities and the damages were categorized as G1 to G5, the G5 indicated the maximum damage. The eligible amount of relief to reconstruct damaged houses depended upon the criteria, that is the entire house broken, (for G1 Rs. 8,000, G2 Rs. 15,000, G3 Rs. 30,000, G4 Rs. 45,000 and G5 Rs. 1,50,000), here the equity concept worked, also the rate differed from area to area according to the intensity of the earthquake. The new houses were constructed according to GSDMA guidelines. There were 30 types of models; the people had the freedom of choosing anyone of these 30 models.

The committees are not functioning well now. After the 2001 earthquake committees were formed to carry out relief, rehabilitation work. But they did not have any proper continuous training. Gujarat State Disaster Management Authority did not provide training to them.

No significant role was given to women before the impact of earthquake. Later, the Kutch Mahila Sangathan was promoted by an NGO involving community in the activities connected with disaster preparedness.

Panchayats are not properly involved. When earthquake occurred in the year 2001, the term of the panchayat had been over. During that time they could not conduct the panchayat elections immediately. So the Government, NGOs and INGOs worked through committees drawn from the representatives of the various communities. No proper Early Warning System was in place, but ICT centres were established by NGOs like Setu and Abhiyan. Traditional Panchayat committees are also functioning. They decide all the panchayat activities. The Government of Gujarat encourages communities to select panchayat leaders instead of having them through elections. If panchayat selects a leader unanimously the Panchayat gets incentive moneys which is totally anti-democratic. Caste leadership is dominant in all the villages.

Wherever NGO has sensitized the community, there is a culture of working together with the government. But the Government is not implementing the schemes directly. But most of the drought prone area schemes are implemented through NGOs. Communities have freedom to choose the NGOs. But they have to get the approval from Gram Sabha. Traditional Panchayats are not properly oriented in developmental activities. There is a lack of sensitization among the officials, NGOs and INGOs on Panchayati Raj Institutions. Gujarat State Disaster Management Authority was formed on the lines of Orissa State Disaster

Management Authority (OSDMA). And it concentrates on disaster preparedness. NGOs organize women as self help groups and they involved these groups in developmental activities.

There was no specific attempt to organize Dalits. NGOs like AGHA KHAN implement long term sustainable projects like construction of check dames, promoting micro finance and micro insurance to their livelihoods. As the monsoons start on June 15th every year, the dams should be constructed failing which the rain water will drain. The dams create further problems to the people and also the rain water will be wasted. So the NGOs felt that though it is impossible to get huge labour force immediately, it is better to involve people so that they can get employment. This will help them earn some money. In constructing houses also as the beneficiaries are involved. This ensured the quality of construction.

The Gujarat State Disaster Management Act, 2003 has entrusted with the responsibility by the District Collector to prepare disaster management bill. The district collector has to prepare the District Management Plan. Local authorities like Panchayats, Municipalities, have to develop their own mitigation strategies. As per the act training should be given to the staff of the local authority by the district administration. The District administration has to coordinate with the local government bodies for the implementation of disaster management plan. In reality the power and value of PRIs are not taken into consideration in respect of the above features.

Common Observations: Applicable to All the Four States

Expectation

- There is no downward accountability in all the four State governments, the NGOs, INGOs and elected representatives. On accountability part no one is sensitive. The stakeholders are not serious about downward accountability. Social audit was not at all conducted. There should be a system to uphold downward accountability. The role of Gram Sabha is to be strengthened.

Suggestions

Evolving a Communication System Covering the Entire Coastal Area

- After the super-cyclone disaster in Orissa, all communication systems became ineffective. The HAM technology could have served the purpose of establishing links. So, encouraging people to use HAM technology in disaster prone areas could be insisted.

- Following the tsunami disaster Central Government reportedly has approved a Rs. 125 crore project for setting up a tsunami warning system in the Indian ocean region, which will use the Deportation Assessment and Reporting Technology (DOART). This early warning system for Tsunamis and Storms in the Indian Ocean is already inoperational. While advance technology can certainly prove to be useful in catching early warning signals, the greatest hurdles would be faced in communicating such warnings to the remote costal areas which are the most vulnerable to the disasters. This is because the costal areas, especially, the remote villages that scarcely have neither televisions nor telephones. Hence, the government besides setting up state-of-the-art warning technology must ensure that the villages in the costal areas have adequate communication facilities.
- In India soon after independence we faced a great human earthquake in the influx of refugees following the partition of the country. On one occasion when Mahatma Gandhi was requested to address the refugees at Kurukshetra, he agreed to do so personally by visiting that places. When that was not possible, he was requested to address the refugees through radio. That was the first and the last live broadcast by the Mahatma Gandhi over radio which took place on 12th November, 1947. It is interesting to know about his feelings after he used the medium of radio to reach out to the distressed people. Referring to the radio he said, this is a miraculous medium. I see Shakthi, the miraculous power of God in it. In the 21st century in a well covered and connected world, Gandhi would have expected us to serve people better by using the miraculous powers of space technology, information technology, electronic media and many other channels for faster communication.
- When normal communication fails during disaster resorting to individual communication sets like HAM radio should be encouraged. For this HAM radio specialization should be given by the Government of India. Even during tsunami, all communication systems failed in Andaman and Nicobar Islands. Only through HAM radio condition of the affected people was

intimated. Government should be the main player in all disaster related activities. But it is to be humanized. Government should ensure the availability of satellite phones in all village Panchayats and orientation should be given to the stakeholders on the uses of satellite phones. Connectivity with the government departments like district/taluk/block level has to be created. ICT centres should be established through the panchayats and coordination of all ICTs could be done by the Panchayati Raj Institutions.

- Besides establishing rescue shelters, the community should be involved in designing and construction activities. These cyclone shelters should have all facilities like electricity, toilets, water, etc. It should be disabled-friendly and gender sensitive structure. The ownership of the cyclone shelter should be given to the panchayats. The panchayat should form the cyclone management committees.
- Government, NGO and INGOs could adopt an appropriate technology in designing and construction of cyclone shelters with the community approval. Disaster management committees should be strengthened and the committees should have an organic link with the panchayats. Each Panchayat can prepare micro level planning including disaster management and proper financial assistance should be devolved by the government for its implementation. The role of the district authorities could be to integrate all of its department activities with Panchayati Raj Institutions.

Preparedness to Meet any Eventuality

- Orientation should be given to committees in all aspects starting from preparedness to reconstruction. Special orientation should be given to youth volunteers in reducing vulnerabilities. Establishment of proper linkages from village to district and state levels should be done. There should be coordination among Gram Panchayat President, INGOs and NGOs at Gram Panchayat level. All schemes and programmes should have gender bias. Creation of data base at the village level and dissemination of information by involving the community is important. This data base should be scientific and approved by the Gram Sabha. All programmes and schemes of various agencies should be implemented based on this data base. And that should be routed through panchayats. Forecasting the vulnerability is important. Clearing the access and escape routes and putting sign boards are also equally important.

- Proper and periodical maintenance of pathways, approach roads, drainage system and community buildings are very essential. Creation of other infrastructure facilities and handing them over to the panchayats is important. Creation of community disaster management fund is yet another need. While creating the temporary shelters care should be taken on gender needs of the stakeholders, protecting the self-dignity and the special characteristics of the habitat.

7

Ways and Means to Strengthen Communities and Panchayats in Disaster Management

The past experience shows that Government, INGOs and NGOs have taken number of measures for relief, rehabilitation and reconstruction activities regarding disaster. Based on experience an array of reports have been prepared for dissemination. Very useful recommendations have been made. But there is no proper initiative to make use of all those suggestions. Government structure in Orissa is very weak but bureaucrats in Tamil Nadu are efficient and they are delivering goods. When tsunami struck, decision making powers were decentralized and respective affected District Collectors were given powers to take decisions based on the ground realities. Apart from the District Collectors many officials efficiently worked. In that situation, the local body institutions were sidelined both by Government and NGOs. Not only in Tamil Nadu, the same situation prevailed in Andhra Pradesh and Gujarat also.

People and their assets were damaged due to flood, cyclone, tsunami and earthquake and they are still in the process of rehabilitation and reconstruction. We have already discussed in the previous chapters the role played by the Government, NGOs, INGOs and Gram Panchayats. This chapter gives suggestions to strengthen panchayats and communities in Disaster Management and Mitigation. It is to be noted that assistance could be extended to the affected at any amount. And people must be made to work for their development. The external agencies can work with people in the system created for them. If any institution or organization or group works for them, community's pride and self-respect will be eroded. People should have a feeling that they can manage on their own with support from others. Despite huge loss of lives and livelihoods in the recent disaster, generous support from the donor agencies and Government enabled the communities to overcome the shock and they started rebuilding. They spent huge amounts on relief, rehabilitation and reconstruction process. But this study found that it had not produced the results to the level of investment. The study found that the relief activities were not gender sensitive and equity oriented. It was supply driven and not demand driven. In this situation, the 73rd and 74th Constitutional Amendments envisage the panchayats should strive for the welfare, safety and the prosperity of the villages. According to the 74th Constitutional Amendment Act, the panchayats should prepare the plan for the socio-economic development of the people. While preparing the socio-economic development plans the panchayats could include disaster management as one of its components. As there was no system, structure and procedures at the grassroots level, the resources dumped at that level had not met the felt needs of the community. In this situation, reconstruction could be done by preparing micro plan at the panchayat level. While preparing micro plan, panchayat could make reliable assessments on the nature and the extent of damages caused by the disaster. The environmental norms such as distance from the sea, identification of safe locations, designs, technologies and materials for construction of safe disaster resistance buildings should be considered. It could ensure that all the vulnerables are identified and included so that they get what is due to them from the reconstruction activities. Panchayats could make use of this opportunity to meet long felt needs. For instance, they could develop new connecting roads that didn't exist earlier.

With regard to damage assessment, the Panchayat could identify number of houses damaged and its magnitude. Public buildings (Anganwadi schools, health centres, community halls, Panchayat building, PDS shop, vocational training centres or any other government structures can be used very effectively). Basic services (including drinking water supply, access roads, sewage disposal, drainage, electricity and communication) apart from the physical damages Panchayats should be aware of the damages. Panchayats should take responsibility to assess the damages and accordingly the relief has to be given.

To ensure the rehabilitation for a long-term development the Panchayats must be made to concentrate on the following activities:

(a) Rebuilding livelihoods,
(b) Opportunity for adopting innovative approaches,

(c) Build their sustainable network of village-based economies, and
(d) Use the opportunity to strengthen and improve livelihood among the people of the village.

Through proactive and well-planned rehabilitation work, we can reduce gender based, caste-based, religion-based, class-based divisions in relief and rehabilitation activities.

A few well trained, well oriented gram panchayat presidents took effects in relief rehabilitation and reconstruction activities. This yielded good results. Based on the field experience, this study suggested the following recommendations to strengthen the community and Panchayats.

At every gram panchayat, Disaster Management Committee headed by gram Panchayat presidents is to be formed. Government should form disaster management committees as statutory committees. In such disaster management committee SHGs, Youth and Elders should be integrated and they have to be oriented. At every ward, a sub-committee at village level headed by ward member has to be constituted. Integrating Disaster Management Training with Panchayat Raj Capacity building exercise should be carried out regularly. In every committee women and Dalit representatives should be incorporated.

Allocation of separate Contingency fund for Disaster Management for every gram panchayat is an imperative. Government should allocate Rs. 1 lakh as untied fund every year to each Gram Panchayat for disaster preparedness and management activities. There should be synergy between the constitutional panchayats and traditional panchayats.

For all relief activities, the government departments have to rely on the committees constituted at the grassroots. A new culture has to be created at the ground to involve people. It requires a special training at all levels from Gram Sabha members to higher officials at district and state level. At every gram panchayat a contingency plan has to be developed. At every block and at every district, plan has to be prepared and implemented with the active participation of the stakeholders.

Panchayats have to take responsibility from the stage of assessment of the loss to reconstruction. Panchayats should have contingency fund. In the same way, every gram panchayat should have food stock through every ration shop. All the physical infrastructure created through various government departments have to be handed over to the panchayats during the period of disaster.

Every state should have a Disaster Management Act, policy and clear-cut guidelines to carry out relief, rehabilitation and reconstruction works. Role clarity has to be ensured. Clear-cut guidelines have to be prepared for disaster management at the gram panchayat level.

As the drought, flood and other disasters are now frequently occurring, each state should have a department meant for disaster relief with sufficient authority. In the regular development activities preparedness component has to be incorporated consciously. A well-maintained communication system has to be developed. With regard to data on the loss and compensation, the panchayat should be held responsible. Gram Panchayat should be made responsible for collecting vital statistics. It has to update the data regularly. This data should be validated by the Gram Sabha. The data have to be confirmed in the Gram Sabha meeting. All relief and rehabilitation activities will be carried out only based on the data already confirmed.

Currently, we need people-centred approach. It should be community-based intervention. Involvement of Constitutional local bodies is more important. All reconstruction activities should be carried out with the support of Village micro plan. Building confidence among people to organise and respond to disaster is also essential.

Based on the 73rd Constitutional Amendment, Panchayats are established as institutionalized structure both in urban and rural areas. But, people are in the periphery. Empowering the people is the process if we include local bodies in the disaster management. This could be a much more profitable system. Usually context decide. As already seen in this study, the empowered and sensitized Panchayat leaders delivered services even during disasters. So Panchayats are the best deliverable institutions where they are not target oriented. They are working in a demand driven way. If we empower Panchayats and the reverse the supply driven process by way of demand driven process, the whole system and society will change for better. Institutionalized, efficient, well coordinated, participatory inclusive, gender sensitive, disaster management initiatives are the basic ingredients of good governance.

Appendix I

Disaster History of India

Cyclones

Year	Events	Death Toll
1737	Calcutta Cyclone	3,000
1839	Coringa Cyclone	3,00,000
1864	Calcutta Cyclone	60,000
1942	Bengal Calcutta Cyclone	40,000
1971	Bengal Orissa Cyclone	9,658
1972	Andhra Pradesh, Orissa	100
1977	Andhra Pradesh Cyclone, Chennai and Kerala	14,202
1979	Andhra Pradesh	594
1981	Gujarat	470
1982	Gujarat, Maharashtra	500
1984	Tamil Nadu, Andhra Pradesh	512
1985	Andhra Pradesh	5,000
1990	Andhra Pradesh, Orissa	1207
1992	Tamil Nadu, Kerala and Karnataka	497
1993	Tamil Nadu and Pondy	—
1996	Andhra Pradesh Cyclone	2,500
1998	Maharashtra, Gujarat Cyclone	2,871
1999	Orissa Kendrapara Cyclone and Andhra Pradesh	10,089
2007	Cyclone Sidr (Bangladesh and India), Cyclone Yemyin—Pakistan, Afghanistan and India	5,303
	Total	**1,56,503**

Earthquakes

Year	Events	Death Toll
1934	Bihar Earthquake	10,700
1935	Quetta Earthquake (British India)	60,000
1950	Arunachal Pradesh-China Border	
1956	Anjar, Gujarat	
1967	Konyna, Maharashtra	
1975	Kinnaur, Himachal Pradesh	
1988	Manipur-Myanmar Border, Bihar-Nepal Border	

(Contd.)

Year	Events	Death Toll
1991	Uttarkashi—Uttar Pradesh Hills	
1993	Latur, Maharashtra	9,748
1997	Jabalpur, Madhya Pradesh	38
1999	Chamoli, Uttar Pradesh	106
2001	Bhuj, Gujarat	13,805
2005	Muzaffarabad (Pakistan) Impact in Jammu and Kashmir	87,350
	Total	**1,81,747**

Famine

Year	Events	Death Toll
1876-1879	Southern Indian Famine	1,00,00,000
1896-1902	Indian Famine	1,90,00,000
1943	Bengal Famine 1943	15,00,000 to 30,00,000
	Total	**3,05,00,000 to 3,20,000**

Floods and Landslides

Year	Events	Death Toll
1961	North	2000
1968	Rajasthan, Gujarat Monsoon Rain	4892
1971	North India	1023
1978	Northern India Monsoon Rain	3800
1980	Uttar Pradesh, Bihar, Gujarat, Kerala and Haryana	1600
1989	Maharashtra, Andhra Pradesh, and Gujarat	1591
1992	Pakistan, Northern India Mansoon Rain—Pakistan, India	1834
1993	South Asian Monsoon Rain—Nepal, India, Bangladesh, Pakistan	3084
1994	Assam, Arunachal Pradesh, Jammu and Kashmir, Himachal Pradesh, Punjab, Uttar Pradesh, Goa, Kerala and Gujarat	2001
1994	Kashmir, Vaundh ghat, Konkan Coast—Landslides	20
1995	Bihar, Haryana, Jammu and Kashmir, Punjab, Uttar Pradesh, West Bengal, and Maharashtra	1479
1995	Aizawl, Mizoram and Kullu, Himachal Pradesh—Landslides	47
1997	Andhra Pradesh, Arunachal Pradesh, Assam, Bihar, Gujarat, Himachal Pradesh, Jammu and Kashmir, Karnataka, Kerala, Maharashtra, Madhya Pradesh,	1442

(Contd.)

Year	Events	Death Toll
	Orissa, Punjab, Rajasthan, Sikkim, Uttar Pradesh, West Bengal	
1998	Assam, Arunachal Pradesh, Bihar, Kerala, Meghalaya, Punjab, Sikkim, Uttar Pradesh, West Bengal	1811
1998	Okhimath, and Malpa, Kali River—Landslides	274
2000	Gujarat, Andhra Pradesh, Assam, Arunachal Pradesh, Bihar, Himachal Pradesh, Kerala, Madhaya Pradesh, Punjab, Uttar Pradesh, West Bengal	1290
August 2003	Uttarkashi—Landslides (Heavy Infrastructure Loss)	—
2004	Eastern India, Bangladesh Monsoon Rain—Bangladesh, India	3076
2005	Mumbai and Surrounding States—Maharashtra, Karnataka, Monsoon Rain	1503
	Total	**32,767**

Extreme Weather

Year	Events	Death Toll
1998	India Heat Wave	2,451
2003	India Heat Wave	1,900
	Total	**4,351**

Hail

Year	Events	Death Toll
9th Century	Roopkund, Uttaranchal	200-600
1888	Moradabad, Uttar Pradesh	246
	Total	**446 to 846**

Tornadoes—Violent Whirlwind

Year	Events	Death Toll
1963	The Assam Tornado	139
1998	The Chakislampur-Goborghata Tornado, India—West Bengal—Orissa	160
	Total	**299**

Tsunami

Year	*Events*	*Death Toll*
1524	Near Dabhol, Maharashtra	Sufficient data not available
2 April, 1762	Arakan Coast, Myanmar	Sufficient data not available
16 June, 1819	Rann of Katch, Gujarat	Sufficient data not available
31 October, 1847	Great Nicobar Island	Sufficient data not available
31 December, 1881	An earthquake of 7.9 in the Entire East Coast of India and Richter scale in Car Nicobar, Andaman and Nicobar Islands 1m tsunamis were recorded at Chennai	Sufficient data not available
26 August 1883	Explosion of the Krakatoa Volcano East Coast of India was affected; in Indonesian. 2m tsunamis were recorded at Chennai	Sufficient data not available
26 June, 1941	An 8.1 Richter scale earthquake in East coast of India was affected the Andaman Archipelago, but no estimates of height of the tsunami is available	Sufficient data not available
27 November, 1945	An 8.5 Richter scale earthquake at West coast of India from north to a distance of about 100km south Karwar was affected; 12m tsunami of Karachi was felt at Kandla	Sufficient data not available
26 December, 2004	Banda Aceh, Indonesia; Tamil Nadu, The East cost of India was affected. Kerala, Andhra Pradesh, Andaman	12,000
	Total	**12,000**

Sources:

1. http:/en.wrkipedia.org/wiki/list_of_natural_disasters_by_death_toll
2. Office of the US Foriegn Disaster Assistance
3. Agricultural Research, Data Book 2002 and 2004
4. Volcanoworld.org
5. Global Volcanism Programme
6. USGS
7. CRED EM-DAT
8. Forces of Nature: World Disasters
9. Epic Disasters: Deadliest Hurricanes

Appendix II

Toba Catastrophe Theory

According to the *Toba Catastrophe Theory*, 70,000 to 75,000 years ago a supervolcanic event at Lake Toba, in Sumatra, reduced the world's human population to 10,000 or even a mere 1,000 breeding pairs, creating a bottleneck in human evolution. The theory was proposed in 1998 by Stanley H. Ambrose of the University of Illinois at Urbana-Champaign.[1, 2]

History

Within the last three to five million years, after human and other ape lineages diverged from the hominid stem-line, the human line produced a variety of species.

According to the Toba Catastrophe Theory a massive volcanic eruption severely reduced the human population. This may have occurred around 70,000-75,000 years ago when the Toba Caldera in Indonesia underwent an eruption of category 8 (or "mega-colossal") on the Volcanic Explosivity Index. This released energy equivalent to about one gigaton of TNT, which is three thousand times greater than the 1980 eruption of Mount St. Helens. According to Ambrose, this reduced the average global temperature by 5 degrees Celsius for several years and may have triggered an ice age.

Ambrose postulates that this massive environmental change created population bottlenecks in the various species that existed at the time; this in turn accelerated differentiation of the isolated human populations, eventually leading to the extinction of all the other human species except for the two branches that became Neanderthals and modern humans.

Evidence

Some geological evidence and computed models support the plausibility of the Toba Catastrophe Theory. The Greenland ice core data displays an abrupt change around this time, but in the corresponding Antarctic data, the change is not easily discernible. Ashes from this eruption of Lake Toba, located near the equator, should easily spread all over the world.

Genetic evidence suggests that all humans alive today, despite their apparent variety, are descended from a very small population, perhaps between 1,000 and 10,000 breeding pairs.[3,4]

Using the average rates of genetic mutation, some geneticists have estimated that this population lived at a time coinciding with the Toba event. These estimates do not contradict the consensus estimates that Y-chromosomal Adam lived some 60,000 years ago, and that Mitochondrial Eve is estimated to have lived 1,40,000 years ago, because Toba is not conjectured to be an extreme bottleneck event, where the population was reduced to one breeding pair.

Gene analysis of some genes shows divergence anywhere from 2 million to 60,000 years ago, but this does not contradict the Toba theory, again because Toba is not conjectured to be a single-pair bottleneck event. The complete picture of gene lineages (including present-day levels of human genetic variation) allows the theory of a Toba-induced human population bottleneck.[5]

Lice Genes Confirm Key Events in Human Evolution

Alan Rogers, a co-author of this study and Professor of Anthropology at the University of Utah, says: "The record of our past is written in our parasites." Rogers and others have proposed the bottleneck may have occurred because of a mass die-off of early humans due to a globally catastrophic volcanic eruption. The analysis of lice genes confirmed that the population of *Homo sapiens* mushroomed after a small band of early humans left Africa sometime between 150,000 and 50,000 years ago.[6]

Migration

According to this theory, humans once again fanned out from Africa after Toba when the climate and other factors permitted. They migrated first to Arabia and India and onwards to Indochina and Australia (Ambrose, 1998, p. 631), and later to the Middle East and what would become the Fertile Crescent following the end of the Würm Glaciation Period (70,000-10,000 years bp).

REFERENCES

1. Ambrose, Stanley H. (1998). "Late Pleistocene Human Population

Bottlenecks, Volcanic Winter, and Differentiation of Modern Humans". *Journal of Human Evolution* 34 (6): 623-651. doi:10.1006/jhev.1998.0219.
2. Ambrose, Stanley H. (2005). Volcanic Winter, and Differentiation of Modern Humans. *Bradshaw Foundation.* Retrieved on 2006-04-08.
3. When Humans Faced Extinction. *BBC* (2003-06-09). Retrieved on 2007-01-05.
4. Dawkins, Richard (2004). "The Grasshopper's Tale", *The Ancestor's Tale, A Pilgrimage to the Dawn of Life.* Boston: Houghton Mifflin Company, 416. ISBN 0-618-00583-8.
5. University of Utah (2004, October 5). Of Lice And Men: Parasite Genes Reveal Modern and Archaic Humans Made Contact. *Science Daily.* Retrieved January 17, 2008, from http://www.sciencedaily.com/releases/2004/10/041005075751.htm
6. *Ibid.*

External Links

- Population Bottlenecks and Volcanic Winter
- 1998 article based on News Release regarding Ambrose's Paper
- Homepage of Professor Stanley H. Ambrose
- Toba Volcano, by George Weber
- Article in *The Economist*
- Journey of Mankind by The Bradshaw Foundation—includes discussion on Toba Eruption, DNA and Human Migrations
- Geography Predicts Human Genetic Diversity *Science Daily* (March 17, 2005) — By analyzing the relationship between the geographic location of current human populations in relation to East Africa and the genetic variability within these populations, researchers have found new evidence for an African origin of modern humans.
- Out of Africa—Bacteria, As Well: Homo Sapiens And H. Pylori Jointly Spread Across, The Globe *Science Daily* (February 16, 2007) — When man made his way out of Africa some 60,000 years ago to populate the world, he was not alone: He was accompanied by the bacterium Helicobacter pylori...; illus. migration map.
- Retrieved from "http://en.wikipedia.org/wiki/Toba_catastrophe_theory"

Appendix III

Most Hazard Prone Districts in India

Sl. No.	*Phase*	*District*	*State*
1.	II	Barpeta	Assam
2.	II	Cachar	Assam
3.	II	Dhemaji	Assam
4.	II	Dhubri	Assam
5.	II	Goalpara	Assam
6.	II	Hailakandi	Assam
7.	II	Kamrup	Assam
8.	II	Karimganj	Assam
9.	II	Lakhimpur	Assam
10.	II	Marigaon	Assam
11.	II	Nagaon	Assam
12.	II	Nalbari	Assam
13.	II	Araria	Bihar
14.	II	Begusarai	Bihar
15.	II	Darbhanga	Bihar
16.	I	Khagaria	Bihar
17.	II	Kishanganj	Bihar
18.	II	Madhepura	Bihar
19.	I	Madhubani	Bihar
20.	II	Munger	Bihar
21.	I	Muzaffarpur	Bihar
22.	II	Patna	Bihar
23.	II	Saharsa	Bihar
24.	II	Samastipur	Bihar
25.	I	Sitamarhi	Bihar
26.	I	Supaul	Bihar
27.	II	Central Delhi	Delhi
28.	II	East Delhi	Delhi

(*Contd.*)

(Contd.)

Sl. No.	Phase	District	State
29.	II	New Delhi	Delhi
30.	II	North Delhi	Delhi
31.	II	North East Delhi	Delhi
32.	II	North West Delhi	Delhi
33.	II	South Delhi	Delhi
34.	II	South West Delhi	Delhi
35.	II	West Delhi	Delhi
36.	I	Amreli	Gujarat
37.	II	Banaskantha	Gujarat
38.	I	Bharuch	Gujarat
39.	I	Bhavnagar	Gujarat
40.	I	Jamnagar	Gujarat
41.		Junagadh	Gujarat
42.		Kutch	Gujarat
43.		Surat	Gujarat
44.	I	Sabarkantha	Gujarat
45.	I	Surendranagar	Gujarat
46.	I	Patan	Gujarat
47.		Porbandar	Gujarat
48.		Rajkot	Gujarat
49.		Vadodara	Gujarat
50.	I	Kolhapur	Maharashtra
51.	I	Latur	Maharashtra
52.	I	Mumbai	Maharashtra
53.	I	Mumbai (Suburban)	Maharashtra
54.	I	Nasik	Maharashtra
55.	I	Osmanabad	Maharashtra
56.	I	Pune	Maharashtra
57.	I	Raigarh	Maharashtra
58.	I	Ratnagiri	Maharashtra
59.	I	Satara	Maharashtra
60.	I	Sindhudurg	Maharashtra
61	I	Thane	Maharashtra
62.	I	Ahmednagar	Maharashtra
63.	I	Dhule	Maharashtra
64.	I	East Garo Hills	Meghalaya
65.	I	East Khasi Hills	Meghalaya
66.	I	Jaintia Hills	Meghalaya
67.	I	Ri Bhoi	Meghalaya

(Contd.)

(*Contd.*)

Sl. No.	*Phase*	*District*	*State*
68.	I	South Garo Hills	Meghalaya
69.	I	West Garo Hills	Meghalaya
70.	I	West Khasi Hills	Meghalaya
71.		Balasore	Orissa
72.		Bhadrak	Orissa
73.		Cuttack	Orissa
74.		Ganjam	Orissa
75.		Jagatsinghpur	Orissa
76.		Jajpur	Orissa
77.		Kendrapara	Orissa
78.		Khordha	Orissa
79.		Koraput	Orissa
80.	I	Nayagarh	Orissa
81.		Nuapada	Orissa
82.		Puri	Orissa
83.	I	Sambalpur	Orissa
84.		Rayagada	Orissa
85.	I	East	Sikkim
86.	I	North	Sikkim
87.	I	South	Sikkim
88.	I	West	Sikkim
89.	II	Chennai	Tamil Nadu
90.	II	Cuddalore	Tamil Nadu
91.	II	Kancheepuram	Tamil Nadu
92.	II	Kanyakumari	Tamil Nadu
93.	II	The Nilgiri	Tamil Nadu
		Nagapattinam	Tamil Nadu
94.	II	Thiruvallur	Tamil Nadu
95.	II	Bahraich	Uttar Pradesh
96.	II	Balrampur	Uttar Pradesh
97.	II	Bijnor	Uttar Pradesh
98.	II	Budaun	Uttar Pradesh
99.	II	Deoria	Uttar Pradesh
100.	II	Ghazipur	Uttar Pradesh
101.	II	Gonda	Uttar Pradesh
102.	II	Gorakhpur	Uttar Pradesh
103.	II	Rampur	Uttar Pradesh
104.	II	Saharanpur	Uttar Pradesh
105.	II	Sant Kabir Nagar	Uttar Pradesh

(*Contd.*)

(Contd.)

Sl. No.	*Phase*	*District*	*State*
106.	II	Siddharthnagar	Uttar Pradesh
107.	II	Sitapur	Uttar Pradesh
108.	II	Chamoli	Uttaranchal
109.	II	Dehradun	Uttaranchal
110.	II	Nainital	Uttaranchal
111.	II	Pithoragarh	Uttaranchal
112.	II	Rudraprayag	Uttaranchal
113.	II	Tehri Garhwal	Uttaranchal
114.	II	Bageshwar	Uttaranchal
115.	II	Uttarkashi	Uttaranchal
116.	II	Bardhaman	West Bengal
117.	II	Jalpaiguri	West Bengal
118.	II	Kooch Behar	West Bengal
119.	II	Murshidabad	West Bengal
120.	II	Nadia	West Bengal
121.	II	North 24 Parganas	West Bengal
122.	II	Puruliya	West Bengal
123.	II	South 24 Parganas	West Bengal
124.	II	Uttar Dinajpur	West Bengal
125.	II	Maldah	West Bengal
126.	II	Dhalai	Tripura
127.	II	North Tripura	Tripura
128.	II	South Tripura	Tripura
129.	II	West Tripura	Tripura
130.	II	Imphal West	Manipur
131.	II	Imphal East	Manipur
132.	II	Thoubal	Manipur
133.	II	Ukhrul	Manipur
134.	II	Tamenglong	Manipur
135.	II	Churachandpur	Manipur
136.	II	Chandel	Manipur
137.	II	Bishnupur	Manipur
138.	II	Senapati	Manipur
139.	II	Aizawl	Mizoram
140.	II	Lunglei	Mizoram
141.	II	Mamit	Mizoram
142.	II	Sershhip	Mizoram
143.	II	Kolasib	Mizoram
144.	II	Saiha	Mizoram
145.	II	Lawngtiai	Mizoram

(Contd.)

(*Contd.*)

Sl. No.	*Phase*	*District*	*State*
146.	II	Champhai	Mizoram
147.	II	Chanlang	Arunachal Pradesh
148.	II	East Siang	Arunachal Pradesh
149.	II	Papum Pare	Arunachal Pradesh
150.	II	Upper Siang	Arunachal Pradesh
151.	II	West Siang	Arunachal Pradesh
152.	II	Upper Dibang Valley	Arunachal Pradesh
153.	II	Lower Dibang Valley	Arunachal Pradesh
154.	II	Lohit	Arunachal Pradesh
155.	II	Tawang	Arunachal Pradesh
156.	II	Upper Subansiri	Arunachal Pradesh
157.	II	East Kameng	Arunachal Pradesh
158.	II	West Kameng	Arunachal Pradesh
159.	II	Lower Subansiri	Arunachal Pradesh
160.	II	Tirap	Arunachal Pradesh
161.	II	Kumng Kame	Arunachal Pradesh
162.	II	Dimapur	Nagaland
163.	II	Kohima	Nagaland
164.	II	Mokokchung	Nagaland
165.	II	Zunheboto	Nagaland
166.	II	Phek	Nagaland
167.	II	Mon	Nagaland
168.	II	Wokha	Nagaland
169.	II	Tuensang	Nagaland

Appendix IV

Project Study Areas — Maps

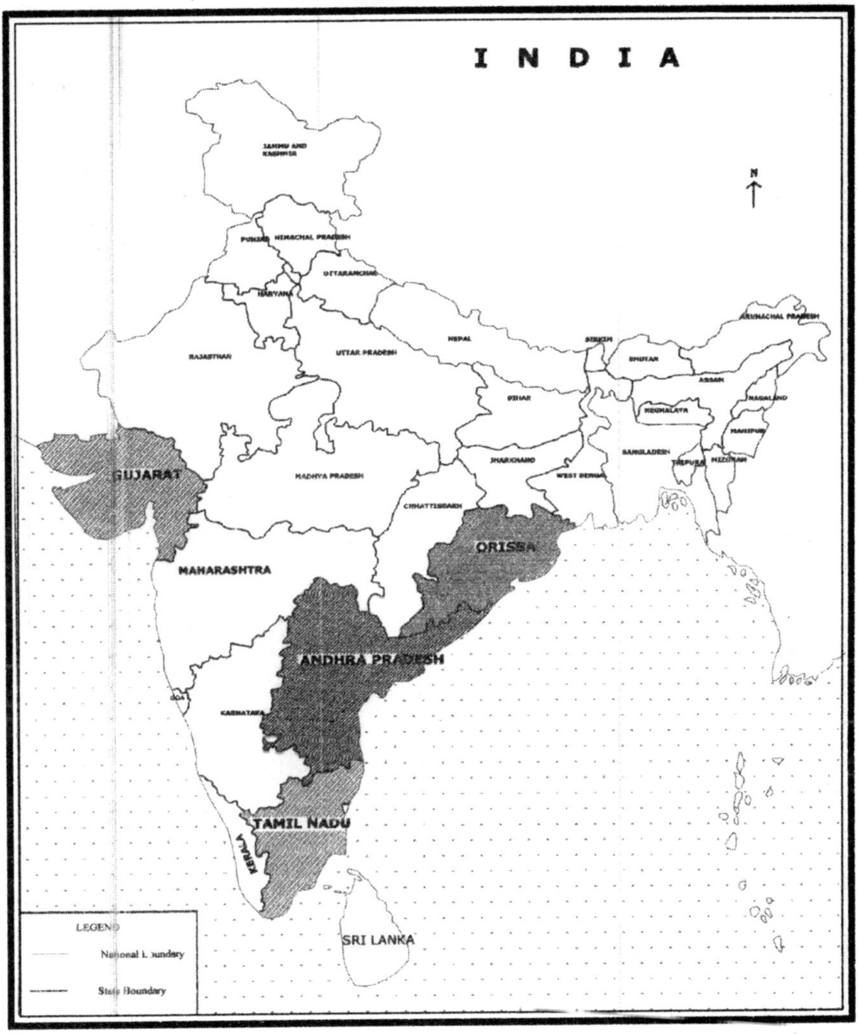

Study Districts in Tamil Nadu

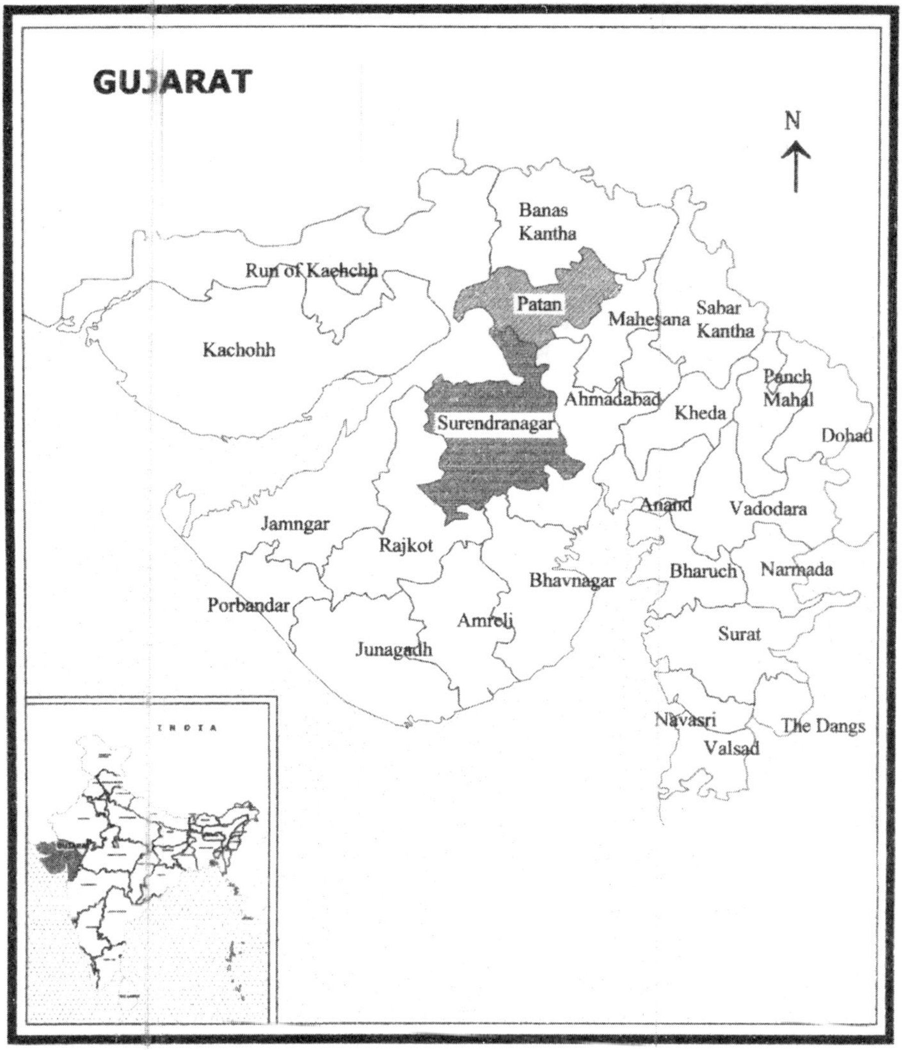

Study Districts in Gujarat

Study Districts in Orissa

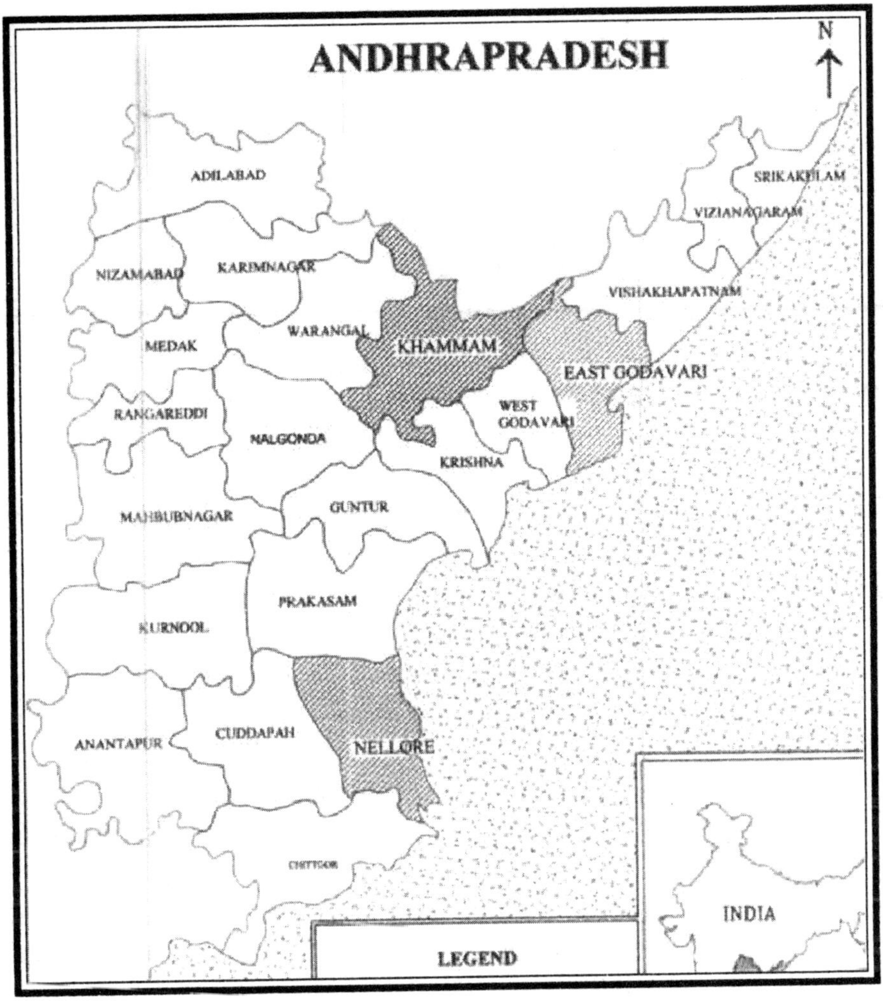

Study Districts in Andhra Pradesh

Bibliography

Abhyan, *Coming Together: A Report on Kutch Earthquake Relief and Rehabilitation Efforts*, (June 2001-March 2003), Kutch: Abhyan, 2003

Action Aid International India, *Disaster Mental Health Care by Medical Officers*, Bangalore: Book for Change, 2004.

Action Aid International India, *Psycho Socio Cure by Community Level Workers for Disaster Survival*, Bangalore: Book for Change, 2004.

Action Aid International India, *Psychological Care for Individuals/Family. Natural Disasters Information Manual-1*, Bangalore: Book for Change, 2004.

Aga Khan Rural Support Programme (India), *Annual Report 2006 on A Programme of the Aga Khan Development Network*, Ahmedabad: Aga Khan Rural Support Programme (India), 2006.

Aga Khan Rural Support Programme (India) Services, *Training and Capacity Building*, Ahmedabad: Aga Khan Rural Support Programme (India) Services, 2006.

Aga Khan Rural Support Programme (India), *Netrang*, Ahmedabad: Aga Khan Rural Support Programme (India) (Tribal Livelihood Resource Centre), 2005.

All India Disaster Mitigation Institute, *Assessing Tsunami Relief: A Community Survey in India, Experience Learning. Series 40*, Ahmedabad: All India Disaster Mitigation Institute, 2006.

Ashoka Trust, *Statement of the CRZ Notification and Post-Tsunami Rehabilitation in Tamil Nadu*, Bangalore: Ashoka Trust for Research in Ecology and the Environment and United Nations Development Programme, 2006.

Asian Development Bank, United Nations and World Bank, *India Post Tsunami Recovery Programme Preliminary Damage and Needs Assessment*, New Delhi: Asian Development Bank, United Nations and World Bank, 2005.

Barooah, M.K., *An Overview of National Disaster Preparedness and Mitigation Programmes*, Dispur: Department of Revenue, Government of Assam, 2006.

Caritas India Newsletter, Issue 31, July 2007.

Catholic Relief Services (CRS), *Miles to go..., Strategy 2011, Rehabilitation and Development*, Chennai: Catholic Relief Resources, 2007.

Centre for Budget and Governance Accountability, *Public Policy Towards National Disasters in India, Disconnect between Resolutions and Reality*, New Delhi: Centre for Budget and Governance Accountability, 2005.

Centre for World Solidarity, *Mainstreaming HIV/AIDS Activities in Disaster Management*, Nagapattinam: Centre for World Solidarity, 2007.

Centre for World Solidarity, *Manual on Safe Fishing*, Nagapattinam: Tsunami Resource Centre, Centre for World Solidarity, 2007.

Centre for Youth and Social Development (CYSD), *A Summary Report on After the Super Cyclone November 1999-October 2000*, Bhubaneshwar: Centre for Youth and Social Development (CYSD), 2001.

Centre for Youth and Social Development (CYSD), *An Interim Report: The Super Cyclone Aftermath: On the Path of Recovery and Restoration*, Bhubaneshwar: Centre for Youth and Social Development (CYSD), 2000.

Centre for Youth and Social Development (CYSD), *Rachana: A Report on School cum Cyclone Shelter Reconstruction*, Bhubaneshwar: Centre for Youth and Social Development (CYSD), 2000.

Centre for Youth and Social Development, *25 years: 1982 –2004: Sowing the Seeds of Change*, Bhubaneshwar: Centre for Youth and Social Development (CYSD), 2007.

Churches Auxiliary for Social Action (CASA), *A Special Edition on Community Based Disaster Preparedness*, Nagapattinam: Churches Auxiliary for Social Action (CASA), 2007.

Concern World Wide India, *The Changing Face of Relief and Rehabilitation Reflection's on the Cuddalore Floods, Tamil Nadu 2005: A New Model?* Chennai, 2006.

Das, Shiva, *On the Shores of Hope*, Madurai: Sadhana Knowledge Systems (A Knowledge Division of the Covenant Centre for Development), 2005.

Das, Subrat, Nandan Kumar Jha, *National Disasters and Relief Provisions in India: Commitments and Ground Realities*, New Delhi: Centre for Governance and Budget Accountability, 2004.

David, Sherine S.A., *UNDP's Disaster Risk Management Programme in Cuddalore District Since Inception*, Cuddalore: DRDA, 2006.

Deustsche Welthungerhilfe e.v., *Tsunami Response Programme 2004-2009*, Chennai: German Agro Action, 2007.

Dhal, Rajeev, Silvio De Curtine, *Experiences in Panchayat-based Planning in the Mountains of Himachal Pradesh*, Shimla: Narrachana, India, 2004.

District Administration, *Disaster Risk Management Programme Cuddalore District, Progress Report: July 2007 to September 2007*, Cuddalore, 2007.

District Administration, *Disaster Risk Management Programme, Activity Carried out from the Inception, Activity Proposed to be Carried out in Current Year 2006-2007*, Cuddalore 2007.

District Collector, *Godavari Flood Manual, Khammam District,* Khammam, Andhra Pradesh, 2007.

District Collector, *Lest we Forget, A Year after Tsunami*, Nagapattinam, 2005.

District Collector, *Two Years of Tsunami, Relief and Rehabilitation: The Kanyakumari Experience,* Nagercoil, 2006.

District Resource Centres in Tsunami Response, Issue: 9, September 2006.

Duryog Nivaram, *Disaster and Vulnerability in South Asia, Programme of Work for Duryog Nivaram,* Colombo: A South Asian Initiative on Disaster Mitigation, 1996.

Environmental Issue, Tamil Nadu Tsunami Resource Centre (TNTRC), *Issue: 7*, July 2006.

Focus on Early Warning System, Tamil Nadu Tsunami Resource Centre (TNTRC), *Issue: 14*, February 2007.

Focus on Environment, Tamil Nadu Tsunami Resource Centre (TNTRC), *Issue: 19*, July 2007.

Focus on Issue of Livelihood, Tamil Nadu Tsunami Resource Centre (TNTRC), *Issue: 5*, April-May 2006.

Focus on Tsunami, Tamil Nadu Tsunami Resource Centre (TNTRC), *Issue: 18*, June 2007.

Gandhi Labour Institute and UNNATI, *Workshop report on Gujarat State Level Consultation on Role of Panchayat Raj Institutions in Disaster Management on May 7, 2002*, Ahemadabed, 2002.

Government of Tamil Nadu and Government of Pondicherry, *India Emergency Tsunami, Reconstruction Project, Environment and Social Management Framework*, (Prepared in Association with the World Bank), April 8, 2005, Chennai, 2005.

Government of Tamil Nadu and UNDP, *Guidelines for Retrofitting of Building,* Chennai, 2006.

Government of Tamil Nadu and UNDP, *Training Manual on Early Warning: Use and Practices*, Chennai, 2006.

Government of Tamil Nadu, *Disaster Management Programme for Teachers*, Chennai: Government of Tamil Nadu, Revenue and Disaster Management and Mitigation Department, 2005.

Government of Tamil Nadu, *Training Manual: Early Warning Use and Practices*, Chennai: United Nations Development Programme and The Office of the Principal Commissioner and Commissioner of Revenue Administration, Revenue Administration Disaster Management and Mitigation Department, Government of Tamil Nadu, 2006.

Habitat International Coalition and PDHRE, Peoples Movement for Human Rights Learning, International Human Rights Standards on Post-Disaster Resettlement and Rehabilitation in Collaboration with the United Nations Special Rapporteur on Adequate Housing, Working Document—January 2006.

Issue on Case Studies and Best Practices, Tamil Nadu Tsunami Resource Centre (TNTRC), *Issue: 10*, October 2006.

Issue on Community-Based Disaster Management, Tamil Nadu Tsunami Resource Centre (TNTRC), *Issue: 8*, August 2006.

Issue on Eco-SAN, Tamil Nadu Tsunami Resource Centre (TNTRC), *Issue: 4*, February-March 2006.

Kottar Social Service Society, *From Agony to Ecstasy—Tsunami Response*, Nagercoil, 2006.

Kumar, Anindya Sarkar (Ed.), *Evolving Strategies for long term Rehabilitation on Shelter and Habitat Development in the Tsunami Affected Areas of Tamil Nadu*, New Delhi: United Nations Development Programme, 2005.

Kutch Nav Nirman Abhiyan, *Abhiyan's Journey Post the 2001 Earthquake*, Kutch, 2002.

Louis, M., *Tsunami Housing: Is Still a Dream?*, Madurai: Tsunami Relief and Rehabilitation Co-ordination (TRRC), Tsunami Legal Action Committee (TLAC), 2006.

Louis, M., *Tsunami: the Hit and the Affected*, Madurai: People Watch, Tamil Nadu, 2005.

M.S. Swaminathan Research Foundation, *Consultation on Post-Disaster Management and Prevention Strategies* in collaboration with the International Development Research Centre (IDRC), Canada, 13-14 May, 2005, Chennai, 2005.

Media in Disaster, Tamil Nadu Tsunami Resource Centre (TNTRC), *Issue: 13*, January 2007.

Ministry of Home Affairs, *Disaster Risk Management Programme (2002-2007), Community Based Disaster Production and Recovery, Through Participation of Communities and Local Self Governments*, New Delhi: Ministry of Home Affairs, National Disaster Management Division, Government of India, United Nations Development Programme, 2003.

Ministry of Rural Development—Government of India, Commissionarate of Rural Development, Government of Gujarat, DRDA, Kutch, UNDP & Sangeevam, *Reviving Peoples Initiatives in Managing Droughts Kutch Nav Nirman Abhiyan, Drought Proofing Programme*, Kutch: Ministry of Rural Development, Government of India, Commissionarate of Rural Development, Government of Gujarat, DRDA, Kutch, UNDP & Sangeevam, 2003.

Muralidharan, E.M., *Community Based Disaster Preparedness: A Guide for Development Workers on Cyclones and Floods*, Vijayawada: Disaster Mitigation Resource Institute, 2000.

National Coordinating Office and Bangalore Administration Office,

National Consultation on Disaster Management, April 18-19, 2005, Chennai, 2005.

National Institute of Disaster Management, *India Disaster Management Congress, 2006*, New Delhi, 2006.

National Institute of Disaster Management, *National Disaster Management Guidelines, Management of Earthquakes*, New Delhi, 2007.

NGO Coordination and Resource Centre, *Snapshot of Damages Due to Tsunami: Village-wise in Nagapatinam District*, Nagapattinam, 2005.

Orissa State Disaster Mitigation Authority, "*Quarterly News Letter*", October-December 2001, April-June 2002.

Orissa State Disaster Mitigation Authority, *Lessons Learnt Orissa Floods—2001,* Bhubaneshwar: Orissa State Disaster Mitigation Authority, A Government of Orissa Agency, 2001.

Orissa State Disaster Mitigation Authority, *State Disaster Management Policy*, Bhubaneswar: Orissa State Disaster Mitigation Authority, A Government of Orissa Agency, 2007.

Orissa State Disaster Mitigation Authority, *The Concept of Earthquake Resistant Designs for Construction of Buildings,* Bhubaneshwar: Orissa State Disaster Mitigation Authority, A Government of Orissa Agency, 2004.

Orissa State Disaster Mitigation Authority, *The Response*, Bhubaneshwar: Orissa State Disaster Mitigation Authority, A Government of Orissa Agency, 2001.

Oxfam (India) Trust, *Conflict Reduction and Peace Building*, Ahmedabad, 2005.

Oxfam (India) Trust, *Relief to Community-Based Disaster Mitigation, the Making of a Sustainable Livelihoods Programme*, Ahmedabad, 2007.

Oxfam International, *Be that Change.... 50 Years of Oxfam in India,* New Delhi, 2007.

Oxfam International, *Gender and Tsunami, Oxfam Briefing Note*, New Delhi, 2005.

Parish Council/Village Development Council, *Kovalam, 2010 (January 2005-December 2010)*, Kovalam, 2005.

Prepare, *Nests by the Side of Waters: Annual Report 2005*, Chennai, 2006.

Rajiv Gandhi Chair for Panchayati Raj Studies, *Report on the Regional Toolkit Workshop on Citizen's Participation in Local Governance in the Reconstruction Process following Natural Disasters with Special Reference to Tsunami*, Gandhigram: Rajiv Gandhi Chair for Panchayati Raj Studies, Gandhi Gram Rural University, 2005.

Ramesh, R. and Thaddeus, *Impact of Tsunami on the Livelihoods of Coastal Communities*, Nagapattinam: NGO Coordination and Resource Centre, Tamil Nadu, 2005.

Reynolds, Tommy, Deepesh Sinha and Sanchit Oza, *Assessing Tsunami Relief: A Community Survey in India, Experience, Learning Series 40*, Ahmedabad: All India Disaster Mitigation Institute, Gujarat, 2006.

Rural Welfare Institute, *Puri District Disaster Response Profile,* Puri, 2007.

Sahayi, *Centre for Collective Learning and Action*, Supported by St. Vances Dependent School, UK, Thiruvananthapuram, 2005.

Sahayi, *Exploring New Visthas*, Thiruvananthapuram, 2006.

Sahayi, *Responding to Emerging Challenges, Sahayi's Interventions and Outcomes, Sahayi Annual Report, 2004-2005*, Thirvananthapuram, 2005.

Samatha Vidya Vyas Vasaya Abhivridhi Samkshem Sangham, *A Brief Activity Report of Samatha Vidya Vyas vasaya Abhivrudhi Samkshema Sangam*, Alamuru, East Godavari District, Andhra Pradesh, 2006.

SCARF (India), *SCARF Commemorative Publication*, Chennai, 2007.

SCARF (India), *Towards a Better Future for the Mentally Disabled*, Chennai, 2007.

SCARF, *Healing Minds*, Chennai, 2007.

Sekhsaria, Pankaj, "New Vulnerabilities: A Changed Topography in the Andaman and Nicobar Islands and Increased Seismic Activity in the Area have to be Factored in for Drafting Appropriate Disaster Responses", *The Hindu*, 23rd December 2007.

Shama, Vinod K., (ed.), *Disaster Management,* New Delhi: Indian Institute of Public Administration, 2006.

Sivanappan and Associates, *Mapping and Study of Coastal Water Bodies in Nagapattinam District*, Nagapattinam: Tamil Nadu Tsunami Resource Centre, 2007.

South Asia Disaster Net, July 2007.

State Institute of Rural Development, Department of Rural Development, *Training Manual in Disaster Management,* Chennai, Tamil Nadu, 2004.

Subash Jeyan, "The Tsunami and the Aftermath: A Village Revisited, Three Years After the Tsunami Struck, A Look at the Way Relief Measures have Shaped up in Pattinacherry, the Worst-Hit Village in the State of Puducherry", *The Hindu*, 23rd December, 2007.

Submitted to Department of Revenue and Disaster Management, Government of Orissa, Civil Society Groups Under the Aegis of Orissa Disaster Mitigation and Management (ODMM), Bhubaneswar, Orissa, *"Recommendation to Civil Society Groups (to be revised as Orissa Disaster Management Code) Revision of Orissa Relief Code"*, 2007.

Tamil Nadu Tsunami Resource Centre, Community Development Organization Trust, *Alcohol Abuse Among the Coastal Communities in Chennai, District Summary Report, 2006*. Chennai: C-Dot, 2006.

Tamil Nadu Tsunami Resource Centre, *On the Shore: NGO Initiatives in Tsunami Response,* Chennai: Tamil Nadu Tsunami Resource Centre, 2006.

Taori, Kamal, *Disaster Management Through Panchayati Raj*, New Delhi: Concept Publishing Company, 2005.

The Disaster Emergency Committee, Member Agencies, Orissa, India, *Community Based Disaster Preparedness Manual*, Bhubaneswar: CARITAS, Help Age India, World Vision, International Federation of Red Cross and Red Cross Societies, Oxfam, Care India, Action AID, Christian AID, Save the Children, 2002.

The Disaster Management Bill, 2005, South Asia Disasters Net, 2007.

The Gujarat Government Gazette, 6th March, 2006.

The Hindu, 23rd December, 2007.

Towards Post Tsunami Livelihoods Security for Fishing Community in Tamil Nadu: A Preliminary Proposal for Concern Citizens, 2005.

Trust for Village Self Governance (TVSG), *Managing Disaster: An*

Introductory Guide for Panchayat from a Panchayat, Kuthambakkam, Thiruvallur District, Tamil Nadu, 2007.

Tamil Nadu Dalit Women Movement, Tsunami Aftermath Violation of Human Rights of Dalit Women, Tamil Nadu, India, Report of the Survey of Women's Human Rights Violation in the Aftermath of the December 20, 2004. Indian Ocean, Tamil Nadu, Asia Pacific Forum of Women Law and Development, 2006.

Asia Pacific Forum of Women Law and Development, *Tsunami Aftermath Violations of Women's Human Rights,* Manila: Thailand, Asia Pacific Forum of Women Law and Development, 2007.

Tsunami Relief and Rehabilitation Coordination (TRRC), *Tsunami Housing: Is Still a Dream*, Madurai: Tsunami Legal Action Committee (TLAC), 2005.

UNDP and Government of Tamil Nadu, *Disaster Management, Training Manual for Village Level People,* Chennai: UNDP, 2004.

UNDP and Government of Tamil Nadu, *Guidelines for Retrofitting of Buildings, Retrofit for Safety,* Chennai: UNDP, 2006.

United Nations Development Programme (UNDP), Cuddalore District, Tamil Nadu, *Disaster Risk Management Programme, Cuddalore District Progress Report*, July 2007-September 2007, Cuddalore: UNDP, 2007.

United Nations Development Programme, *Disaster Preparedness and Response Plan*, New Delhi: United Nations Development Programme, 2006.

United Nations Population Fund and UNNATI, *Gujarat State Level Consultation on Role of Panchayat Raj Institutions in Disaster Management*, Ahmedabad: United Nations Population Fund and UNNATI, 2002.

United Nations Team for Recovery Support, *Tsunami Recovery: A Joint UN Report—India*, Chennai: UNTRS, 2006.

United Nations Team for Tsunami Recovery Support, *Progress Report*, Chennai, 2007.

United Nations Tsunami and Recovery Support, Care, Save the Children, *A joint Report on Turning the Tide-Touching the Lives of the Neglected in Tsunami Recovery,* Chennai: United Nations, 2007.

United Nations, *Recovery Framework in Support of Government of India for a Post Tsunami Rehabilitation and Reconstruction Programme*, January-March 2005, New Delhi, 2005.

United Nations, The World Bank and The Asian Development Bank, *A Joint Report on Tsunami—India—Two Years After*, New Delhi, 2007.

UNNATI, *Annual Report 2006-07 Organization for Development Education*, Ahmedabad, 2007.

Vikash in 2006-2007, Bhubaneswar: Vikash, 2007.

Vinod, R.K. Sharma, *Community-Based Disaster Preparedness, Prevention and Mitigation: Sustainable Approaches*, 2002.

Voluntary Action, News Letter of Sahayi, *Centre for Collective Learning's and Action,* Volume 7 and Number: 3, July-September, 2005.

Online References

www.tn.nic.in.

www.wecanendraw.org

www.undp.org

www.sphereproject.org

www.gsdma.org

www.tntrc.org

www.worldbank.org

www.osdma.org

www.ap.gov.in

www.aponline.gov.in

www.tngovt.in

Index

Index